CULTURE SMART!

FRANCE

Barry Tomalin

Graphic Arts Center Publishing®

First published in Great Britain 2003
by Kuperard, an imprint of Bravo Ltd.

Series Editor Geoffrey Chesler
Design DW Design

Simultaneously published in the U.S.A. and Canada
by Graphic Arts Center Publishing Company
P. O. Box 10306, Portland, OR 97296-0306

Second printing 2003

Library of Congress Cataloging-in-Publication Data

Tomalin, Barry, 1942-
France : a quick guide to customs and etiquette / by Barry Tomalin.
    p. cm.
Includes bibliographical references and index.
ISBN 1-55868-703-3
1. France—Social life and customs. 2. Etiquette—France. 3.
National characteristics, French. I. Title.
DC33.7.T598 2003
944—dc21
                                2002151219

Printed in Hong Kong

Cover image: Stone house in lavender field, Bonnieux, Provence.
Travel Ink/David Forman

CultureShock!Consulting and **Culture Smart!** guides both contribute
to and regularly feature in the weekly travel program "Fast Track"
on BBC World TV.

About the Author

BARRY TOMALIN is a writer and trainer with thirty years' experience
in education and training in France, and lead consultant for
CultureShock!Consulting. He has lived in France, Algeria, and in
Francophone Africa, and has trained business students and diplomats.
Fluent in French, he has a BA in anthropology and linguistics from the
University of London, and is a module leader in the MA program in media,
technology, and culture studies at the University of Westminster in London.

Other Books in the Series

Other titles are in preparation. For more information,
contact: info@kuperard.co.uk

The publishers would like to thank **CultureShock!**Consulting
for its help in researching and developing the concept for this series.

CultureShock!Consulting

We are all likely at some time to be dealing with other cultures—foreign
visitors at home, e-mails from abroad, overseas sales agents, multicultural
teams within our organization, or a new foreign management structure.

CultureShock!Consulting creates tailor-made seminars and consultancy
programs to meet all types of corporate, public sector, and individual
intercultural needs. It provides pre- and post-assignment programs, as well
as ongoing "in-the-field" counseling worldwide.

For details, see www.cultureshockconsulting.com

contents

contents

Map of France

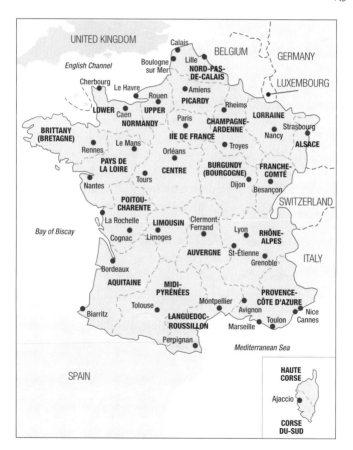

UNITED KINGDOM

English Channel

Cherbourg
Le Havre
Rouen
Caen
LOWER **UPPER**
NORMANDY
BRITTANY
(BRETAGNE)
Rennes
Le Mans
PAYS DE
LA LOIRE
Nantes
Tours
POITOU-
CHARENTE
La Rochelle
Cognac
Bordeaux

Calais
Boulogne
sur Mer
Lille
NORD-PAS-
DE-CALAIS
Amiens
PICARDY
Paris
Rheims
CHAMPAGNE-
ARDENNE
IIE DE FRANCE
Orléans
Troyes
CENTRE
BURGUNDY
(BOURGOGNE)
Dijon
Besançon

BELGIUM
GERMANY
LUXEMBOURG

LORRAINE
Strasbourg
Nancy
ALSACE
FRANCHE-
COMTÉ

SWITZERLAND

LIMOUSIN
Limoges
Clermont-
Ferrand
Lyon
RHÔNE-
ALPES
AUVERGNE St-Étienne
Grenoble

ITALY

Bay of Biscay

AQUITAINE
MIDI-
PYRÉNÉES
Tolouse
Biarritz
LANGUEDOC-
ROUSSILLON
Perpignan
Montpellier
Avignon
PROVENCE-
CÔTE D'AZURE
Toulon
Marseille
Nice
Cannes

Mediterranean Sea

SPAIN

HAUTE
CORSE
Ajaccio
CORSE
DU-SUD

introduction

The French are "different." You'll often hear this in conversations among the "Anglo-Saxons," as the French like to call English-speakers. "Different" means charming, challenging, uncooperative, questioning, and doing things in their own way and to their own advantage.

So what makes them so distinctive? And how do you get through to them? What is obvious is that the French have a keen sense of national identity, which comes from their history and their language. France was a considerable colonial power, with interests around the world. French was the language of international diplomacy from the seventeenth to the nineteenth centuries. The French Revolution changed the course of history. Above all, France sees herself as one of the foremost contributors to civilized life—through her cuisine, her monuments, her authors, artists, composers, scientists, explorers, and mathematicians. No list of world literature can be compiled without French names in it, and few other countries contain such regional richness, both cultural and physical. France's continuing cultural influence is due largely to her consistent attempt to dominate the intellectual high ground, reflecting an insistence on logical thought, and a love of philosophical speculation.

France punches above her weight in world affairs, and carefully guards her interests and prestige, often in opposition to world opinion. Yet the French are constantly asking what it means to be French, even while asserting their difference from and essential superiority to all other nations.

For many foreigners, the essence of Frenchness is their commitment to their quality of life. To be French means knowing instinctively where work ends and pleasure begins, and never allowing the one to take over the other. Indeed, the idea that the French may become workaholics inspires deep dismay among sympathetic observers.

By looking at the attitudes and values of the French, and explaining how French life and business works, *Culture Smart! France* shows you how to fit in as a foreigner. It gives practical advice on how to avoid the pitfalls and how to do things the French way, and to get results as you do so. It takes you through French history, festivals and traditions, the French at home, on the road, in the restaurant, and at work. The French in love we leave to your imagination! Above all, we show you how the French communicate, and how to get the best out of this utterly frustrating yet totally charming and brilliant people.

Key Facts

Official Name	République Française. France is a full member of NATO and of the European Union, and one of the five permanent members of the UN security council.
Capital city	Paris. Population 9.8 million
Main cities	Lyon, Marseille, Lille, Toulouse, Bordeaux.
Area	210,026 sq. miles (543,965 sq. km.)
Climate	Temperate, varying with terrain, to Mediterranean in the south.
Currency	Euro. The Franc was replaced by the Euro on January 1, 2002.
Population	59 million
Ethnic make-up	86 percent French, of Celtic and Latin descent. Basque minority in the southwest. 14 percent foreign (including other EU nationals and North African immigrants)
Language	French. Regional languages include Basque, Breton, Catalan, and Provençal.
Religion	Roman Catholic 90% Muslim 5% Protestant 2% Jewish 1% Other 2%

Government	A unitary republic with an elected President and an elected Prime Minister. Two houses of Parliament, the Assemblée Nationale, and the Sénat. France is a multiparty democracy.	Metropolitan France is divided into twenty-two regions, containing ninety departments. There are four overseas departments, two territorial collectivities, and four overseas territories
Media	France has a number of state radio and television channels, supplemented by a variety of commercial channels.	Both a national and a regional press. The best-known newspapers are *Le Monde, Le Figaro,* and *La France à la Une.*
Media (English language)	*Le Monde* carries a weekly English-language supplement from the *New York Times.*	
Electricity	110 volts or 220 volts. Two-prong adaptors are used. Adaptors needed for U.S. appliances.	
Video/TV	SECAM system	NTSC TV does not work in France.
Telephone	France's country code is 33. To dial out of France, dial 00.	

chapter one

LAND & PEOPLE

"*Douce France
Cher pays de mon enfance.*"

"Gentle France, dear country of my childhood."
So sang the French crooner Charles Trenet in
1943. Sixty years on, and the gentle charms of
France continue to enchant.

GEOGRAPHICAL SNAPSHOT

France is the largest country in Western Europe
after Russia—210,026 sq.
miles (543,965 square
kilometers), including
Corsica—and in spite of a
population of 59 million,
it feels less crowded than
other European countries.
Seventy-five percent of
the population live in the

major cities, but 25 percent still live in the country,
and regional culture is still very strong.

Geographically, France extends from the rolling plains of the north and east, and the high plateau in the Massif Central, to the hilly south and the Mediterranean paradise of the Côte d'Azur; from the mountain ranges of the Jura and the Alps in the east to the Atlantic Ocean in the west, and the Pyrenees in the southwest. It is hexagonal in shape. "*L'Héxagone*," "*La France Métropolitaine*," and "*La Métropole*" are three ways in which French people refer to their country to distinguish it from the overseas *Départements d'Outre Mer* (DOM) or the *Territoires d'Outre Mer* (TOM).

The four DOM are Martinique, Guadeloupe, French Guiana, and l'Isle de la Réunion. The TOM are Mayotte in the Indian Ocean, New Caledonia, Wallis and Futuna and French Polynesia in the Pacific, the French Antarctic territories and St. Pierre et Miquelon off the coast of Canada. These bear testimony to the variety and diversity of France's former overseas empire. Nearly two million French citizens live abroad, of whom a million live elsewhere in Europe and half a million in the United States.

It is also important to remember that France retains close contacts with its former French-speaking colonies in North Africa, notably Algeria, Tunisia, and Morocco; in West Africa, notably Senegal, the Ivory Coast, and Cameroon; and Indochina, notably Vietnam and Laos.

Within metropolitan France itself live some four million foreign nationals, of whom 1.5 million are European Union nationals. France accounts for 16 percent of the total population of the European Union.

Focusing on the metropolitan area, France is bordered in the west by the Channel (in French, *La Manche*) and the Atlantic Ocean, and in the southeast by the Mediterranean. She is separated from Spain by the Pyrenees (literally "born of fire"), and from Switzerland and Italy by the Alps and the Jura. In the east, the River Rhine separates France from Germany. Only in the northeast are there no natural frontiers separating France from Luxembourg, Germany, and Belgium. France boasts Europe's highest mountain, Mont Blanc (15,771 feet, or 4,867 meters).

Rivers as well as mountains provide an easy way of situating a town or area. There are five main rivers, or *fleuves*. Paris is on the River Seine.

The Loire is famous for its Renaissance châteaux, and was the heart of French civilization in the sixteenth century. The Rhine in the east separates the province of Alsace from the Black Forest in Germany, and was for a long time a bitterly disputed territory between the two countries. Strasbourg, home of the European Parliament, in Alsace, now symbolizes a new era of peace. The Rhône comes from Switzerland through Lake Geneva, changes direction at Lyon, and then flows south. Marseille is situated on its Mediterranean delta. In English, Marseille is spelled Marseilles, a source of puzzlement for the French, for whom the "s" marks the plural. Finally, the Garonne flows from Spain toward Toulouse, where it turns northwestward to flow toward the Atlantic. Bordeaux lies on its estuary, the Gironde.

Cities

France's six main cities are Paris, the capital, in the north, and Lyon, Marseille, Lille, Toulouse, and Bordeaux. Paris itself has a population of about ten million, but none of the other major cities has a population of more than 1.5 million.

Climate

France is blessed overall with a temperate climate, but because of its size and topography there are variations between the extreme summer heat on the Mediterranean in the south and the icy cold of the Alps in the southeast in winter. Basically, there are three types of climate: oceanic in the west, where France borders the Atlantic Ocean; continental in the east and in the interior of the country and in Paris; and Mediterranean in the south. In the north and west temperatures don't vary enormously, due to the influence of the Gulf Stream. In Paris, for example, temperatures range from 37° F (3° C) in January to 70° F (23° C) in July and August. In the south the differences are greater. The weather is mild in winter, but in summer can be unbearably hot and dry, with risks of drought and forest fires. The best traveling months are May, June, September, and October.

The Mistral

Of particular interest is the mistral, a seasonal wind that blows across the Mediterranean from the Sahara in winter and spring and which affects the mood of the population. It is a heavy, cold, dry, sand-laden wind that can travel at around 60 mph (nearly 100 kmph) and blow for days at a time. People in the south often complain of depression when the mistral is blowing. The number of suicides is even claimed to rise during the mistral period.

Administration

France is marked by a high degree of centralization and hierarchy, based in Paris, despite attempts to decentralize power to the regions between 1972 and 1986. France is divided into 100 *départements* (departments), of which ninety-six are in the *Métropole* and four in the DOM.

The *départements* are grouped into twenty-six larger administrative regions (twenty-two in the *Métropole* and four in the DOM). *Départements* are ordered alphabetically, and numbered. The numbers are used as postal codes and also as identification on car registration numbers. So on a car registration number, the last two digits, 75, stand for Paris, and a letter addressed to 75006 Paris will be delivered to an address in the sixth *arrondissement* (district) in Paris.

Départements were introduced after the French Revolution in 1789, but most French people will identify themselves by the name of their region, such as Brittany, Normandy, Alsace, or Provence. The regional name immediately brings to mind a type of landscape, climate, tradition, cooking, and way of speaking. The French regions retain a  great variety of culture, customs, and wine-making and culinary traditions.

As in other countries, there is a difference between north and south in France. Northerners reckon that *les gens du midi* (southerners) talk and boast a lot, are expansive, make friends easily but rather superficially, have little sense of time, and never hurry. The southerners reckon that *les gens du nord* (northerners) are cold, hardworking, not sociable, and difficult to make friends with—but when friendships are formed they are lifelong.

THE FRENCH: A BRIEF HISTORY

Brief is hardly a word to apply to French history, which has had an unparalleled influence on world thought and culture. It is worth remembering that for three centuries French was the international language of diplomacy and intellectual exchange; that France had a huge empire, with outposts in America, India, the Far East, Africa, and the Caribbean as late as 1960; that English is imbued with words of French origin; and that the American War of Independence was supported by French troops and sparked France's own epochal revolution in 1789. French philosophers, writers, artists, and musicians, such as Descartes, Pascal, Rousseau, Voltaire, Sartre, Renoir, Matisse, Bizet, and Debussy, are part of the world's cultural currency, and French filmmakers uphold a tradition of cutting-edge creativity.

The Romans

France was one of Europe's earliest unified countries. The original Celtic inhabitants were known collectively as the Gauls. There were some four hundred different tribes, speaking over seventy-two different languages. Over a series of campaigns, the Roman Emperor Julius Caesar finally succeeded in pacifying the Gauls in 51 BCE. He described these in his *Gallic Wars*, and one of his sentences, "I came, I saw, I conquered," has become famous. One of modern France's most ingenious comic creations has been Astérix the Gaul, the plucky little Celt whose village outwits the stupid Romans every time and whose language is a wonderful mix of Latin and modern French. His expression of amazement "*Ils sont fous, ces Romains!*" ("They're crazy, these Romans!") became a catchphrase. Parc Astérix, north of Paris, is a patriotic theme park equivalent to Disneyland.

Some say that Julius Caesar actually wanted to become a commander on the Danube in central Europe and not in the provincial backwaters of France, but was attracted west by the prospect of local gold to pay off his huge debts. Roman rule in France established the Latin language, a version of which was to become modern French, and also imposed a uniform system of law.

Many Roman ruins can still be seen, especially in the south. There is the Pont du Gard aqueduct in Arles, the bullfighting arena in Nîmes, and the Musée de Cluny in the Latin Quarter of Paris, sited in an old Roman bathhouse.

From Clovis to Charlemagne

After Rome finally withdrew in the fifth century CE, France was conquered by the Franks, Germanic tribes originally from Pomerania, on the Baltic. Clovis, the first Frankish king to become a Christian, was baptized in Rheims in 498/9. The Franks dominated Western Europe for more than three centuries.

Clovis's successors, the Merovingian dynasty, tended to leave the administration to their bishops and counts, drawn from the Gallo-Roman aristocracy. Among the powerful families acting as the king's agents—holding office as mayors of the royal palace—was Charles Martel, "the Hammer." He succeeded in beating back the Moorish invasion at Poitiers in 732, and subsequently established a new ruling dynasty. His son, Pepin the Short, usurped the Frankish throne, thereby establishing the Carolingians, and Pepin's son, Charlemagne (Charles the Great) became a great pan-European monarch.

Charlemagne was crowned Holy Roman Emperor on Christmas Day 800 in Rome. The Frankish Empire included the Lombard kingdom of Italy, large parts of Germany, and a march (boundary province) across the Pyrenees in northern Spain. The Empire fell apart after his death, but from the  time of Charlemagne the three ethnic roots of the French people, Frankish, Celtic, and Roman, fused to form a single nation. Weak central government, however, allowed the great nobles to become virtually independent of the monarch. Under a Frankish institution, the "Salic law," women were barred from reigning or passing on the right to the throne. This would become the cause of significant Franco-British rivalry. However sexist and backward the Salic law may seem today, it is worth remembering that Charlemagne, who was illiterate himself, also made education compulsory for children.

Franco-British Rivalry
France and Britain, as might be expected from two nations separated by a strip of water twenty-two miles wide, have clashed on a number of occasions. One reason is that English kings,

since the eleventh century, had designs on the westernmost parts of France.

Julius Caesar had invaded Britain from France in 55 BCE, and the next major conquest was that of William, Duke of Normandy, in 1066 CE. From that point on, the Anglo-Norman monarchs held claims to great swathes of land in France. During the Hundred Years War between England and France, from 1337 to 1453, the inspired leader of French resistance, Joan of Arc, was sold to the English and burned at the stake in Rouen in 1431. English claims to French soil were only really settled when the English military and civilian administration was withdrawn from Normandy after the battles of Formigny in 1450 and Castillon in 1453. Even so, England only finally gave up Calais in 1558.

In the following centuries, France harbored claimants to the English throne such as Mary, Queen of Scots, Charles II, and James Stuart (Bonnie Prince Charlie). This rivalry grew with the formation of the great European empires. By the seventeenth century, France had become the leading power in Europe, with colonies and trading posts around the world. In the Seven Years War (1756–63) she lost most of her colonies in

India and Canada to Britain. As late as 1940, when Britain celebrated the successful evacuation of 300,000 British troops from Dunkirk in the face of the invading Germans, the French lamented this as a cynical betrayal that left a mere 40,000 French troops to face the German army. A major London railway station, Waterloo, commemorates the defeat of the "dictator Napoleon" in 1815. A major Paris railway station, the Gare d'Austerlitz, commemorates the Emperor Napoleon's famous victory in 1805, after which, in 1806, he abolished the German-dominated Holy Roman Empire.

Catholicism and Protestantism

Although France has no official religion, the country is 90 percent Roman Catholic. In the second half of the sixteenth century, civil wars between nobles were fought under religious banners, Catholic versus Protestant (or Huguenot, as they were called). France has had only one Protestant king, Henri de Navarre, who as Henri IV became the first king of the Bourbon dynasty. He established peace, having converted to Catholicism in order to ascend the throne. His words, "Paris is worth a mass," have echoed down the centuries. After the bloody European wars of religion, Henri IV guaranteed the

Protestants freedom of worship and personal security. In 1610 he was assassinated by a Catholic fanatic, who stabbed him in the eye.

In subsequent years Protestant rights were progressively eroded until, in 1685, with the revocation of the Edict of Nantes by Louis XIV, these were officially withdrawn. This led to the mass emigration of about 400,000 Huguenots, who took their industrial skills to the Netherlands, to Britain, to Germany, to South Carolina, to Canada, and even to distant southern Africa. In some of the Loire châteaux, underground passages still exist leading from the castles to the port of Nantes, where boats were moored to aid the Huguenots in their escape.

In 1764, persecution became less stringent in exchange for greater leniency toward French Catholic settlers in Canada, and after the American War of Independence, Jefferson and Lafayette obtained official tolerance for French Protestants in 1788.

In 1797 the egalitarian ideals of the French Revolution were finally realized, and religious discrimination was ended in France. In 1802 the Huguenot Church was again officially recognized. The Republican motto "*Liberté, Egalité, Fraternité*" ("Liberty, Equality, Fraternity") adorns monuments, coins, schools, and town halls throughout France to this day.

The Bourbon Monarchy

France's greatest monarch was Louis XIV, "the Sun King," who reigned for nearly seventy-three years, from 1643 until 1715. While England was undergoing a civil war, and the execution of its king, Charles I, Louis XIV became an absolute monarch, ruling by "divine right." He defeated a revolt of his own nobles, supported by the people of Paris, in a civil war called the Fronde, and emerged with total control over the country, with power centered on himself and his magnificent palace at Versailles. He was a patron of the arts, and presided over a golden age of French art, science, and letters. This was the great age of French classical drama, of Corneille, Racine, and Molière, whose plays are still performed in traditional style at the Comédie Française theater in Paris. Under Louis XIV French culture became the model for all of civilized Europe.

The Sun King's frivolous and profligate successor, Louis XV, let affairs drift and sought escape in sensuality. Government became more arbitrary and aimless, and a series of long wars brought the country close to bankruptcy. He was famous for his mistresses, one of whom, Madame de Pompadour, was effectively prime minister for almost twenty years.

His successor was the well-meaning but weak Louis XVI, who was deposed during the French

Revolution and executed in 1793, followed in the same year by his wife, the Austrian princess Marie Antoinette. Their son, Louis XVII, the Dauphin, died of illness in the Temple prison in Paris in 1795.

The French Revolution, 1789–99

The Revolution of 1789 was the turning point in French history. In May of that year, Louis XVI called a meeting of the long-dormant Estates-General (the French parliament) at Versailles in order to discuss reform of the state finances. At that meeting, exasperated by his failure to grasp the nettle of poverty and economic instability and to recognize the aspirations of the rising urban middle class, the representatives of the third of the three "estates" (nobles, clergy, and commons) unilaterally declared themselves a National Assembly and took the famous "tennis court oath" to draw up a new constitution.

Rumors of royal plans to break up this Assembly led to riots in Paris and the storming of the Bastille prison, symbol of Bourbon despotism. The army joined the revolutionaries, and the relatively restrained constitutional revolt was thus overtaken by a mass movement that swept away the old order, and led to the creation of a democratic republic. The French Revolution is commemorated on Bastille Day on July 14.

The Assembly abolished the feudal system and published a "Declaration of the Rights of Man and of the Citizen." In order to bring in revenue it confiscated Church property, placing the clergy on the state payroll. Local government was reformed, and the separation of legislative, executive, and judicial powers was enshrined in Europe's first written constitution, based on the rational ideas and beliefs developed by the French *philosophes.*

In 1791 the king attempted to flee Paris, but was recaptured. Invasion by Austria and Prussia in support of the monarchy sealed his fate. The government was dismissed, a national convention was elected by universal suffrage, and on September 22, 1792, a republic was declared. Louis was tried for conspiring with the enemy, and was condemned to death.

The Convention was at first divided between relatively moderate Girondists and radical republican Jacobins. In 1793, however, it delegated power to the infamous Committee of Public Safety, led by the Jacobin extremist Robespierre, and a reign of terror began. The use of the guillotine to behead aristocrats and revolutionaries alike has left an indelible series of images on the historical landscape. The instability, violence, and mass executions carried out during the successive revolutionary regimes have also given rise to a number of romantic tales, that of *The Scarlet Pimpernel* being perhaps the best known.

In 1794 Robespierre was himself deposed and executed, and a moderate executive Directory of five members was created. The French desire to export the principles of the Revolution, and the determination of Britain, Austria, and Russia to contain it, led to another European war, and produced one of France's defining figures, Napoleon Bonaparte. In 1799 the Directory was overthrown in a coup d'état, and a Consulate of three was established. The young general Napoleon was appointed First Consul, with special powers.

The Empire of Napoleon
Born in Corsica in 1769, Napoleon Bonaparte had risen through the ranks of the revolutionary army to become its most brilliant general, masterminding a series of stunning victories against the antirevolutionary powers of continental Europe and almost succeeding in invading Britain. The Franco-Spanish fleet was defeated by British

sea power in 1805 at the battle of Trafalgar, off the coast of southwest Spain, in which the British Admiral Lord Nelson died. Not daunted, Napoleon moved immediately to consolidate his land advantages and two months later overwhelmed the Austrians and Russians at Austerlitz. The following year he routed the Prussians at Jena.

Within France, Napoleon restored law and order and made sweeping internal reforms, including the establishment of the Bank of France, and an accommodation, or Concordat, with the Catholic Church. A grateful nation made him Consul for Life in 1802. Two years later, in the presence of Pope Pius VII, he crowned himself Emperor of France in a dramatic ceremony in the cathedral of Notre Dame, thus becoming the symbolic successor to Charlemagne. (It is said that the young Beethoven was so incensed by this action that he tore out the dedication to Napoleon from the manuscript of his *Eroica* symphony.)

From 1799 to 1815, Napoleon dominated Europe, making members of his own family heads of state in various countries. The empire he created in Western Europe, however, was unlike any other, being ruled in accordance with the basic reforms of the French Revolution. It gave its subjects the completely new experience of life under a centralized modern state, and spread the principles of the Revolution even to its enemies.

Unable to overcome Britain's superiority at sea, Napoleon launched an economic campaign against British trade and industry, known as the "continental system." This trade war proved difficult to sustain. Then came his disastrous invasion of Russia in 1812, in which his *Grande Armée* of 600,000 was decimated by the Russia winter, followed by heavy defeats in Germany and Spain, after which the allied armies of Britain, Russia, Austria, and Prussia converged on France in 1814. Napoleon abdicated and was exiled to the island of Elba in the Mediterranean. In 1815 he escaped, landed at Cannes, and made a triumphal march north to Paris. The decisive battle was fought near Waterloo, in Belgium, where the Emperor finally succumbed to a coalition of allied forces under the command of Arthur Wellesley, Duke of Wellington. He died in exile on the island of St. Helena in the south Atlantic in 1821.

Napoleon's great legacy to France lies in the *Code Napoléon*, which consolidated the majority of the legal reforms of the Revolution and remains the basis of French law, and in a certain sense of grandeur, or cultural superiority. He also left his own dynasty. Although the Bourbon monarchy was restored in 1815, it did not last. Reform was in the air—fanned by the political philosophies of revolutionary liberalism and nationalism, by the Romantic idealism fostered by poets and authors, and by the social changes caused by the growing industrial revolution.

In 1830 an armed insurrection in Paris led by liberal printers and journalists deposed the reactionary Bourbon Charles X in favor of his cousin, Louis Philippe, "the citizen king." Louis Philippe's liberal monarchy failed to satisfy democratic demands, however, and in 1848 a further revolution, enshrining universal manhood suffrage, established the Second French Republic. A tidal wave of reform now flooded across Europe.

Within the National Assembly, conflict between liberals and socialists gave the great Napoleon's nephew, Prince Louis-Napoléon Bonaparte, the opportunity to present himself as a unifying national leader. He was elected president in 1848, and in 1852 he proclaimed the Second Empire, taking the title of Napoleon III.

The Second Napoleonic Empire

During Napoleon III's reign, from 1852 to 1870, France prospered, developed, and became again the preeminent power in Europe. Abroad he rebuilt her colonial empire. Toward the end of his reign, however, costly foreign policy mistakes threatened these achievements, and France faced increasing tension with the political unification of Germany under Prussian leadership.

Across the Atlantic, to shore up his waning prestige, in 1862 Napoleon III breached the Monroe doctrine of noninterference in the American sphere of influence by promoting the Archduke Maximilian of Habsburg as emperor of Mexico, in an experiment in democratic imperialism. Maximilian's French troops were soon tied down by the guerrilla tactics of the radical President Benito Juarez, and when the United States, emerging from the Civil War, reasserted its opposition, they were recalled. Maximilian was captured and shot in Mexico City, and Napoleon was left with an expensive humiliation.

Worse was to come in the conflict with Prussia. France was maneuvered into war by the canny Prussian statesman Otto von Bismarck, and was roundly defeated at the Battle of Sedan in 1870, where Napoleon himself was captured. In Paris, news of the disaster led to the proclamation of a new republic, the Third French Republic.

The Paris Commune
In the uncertainty following the defeat at Sedan there was considerable unrest in Paris. German armies now besieged the city, and in 1871

Bismarck inaugurated the new German Empire in a ceremony in the Hall of Mirrors in Louis XIV's palace at Versailles. During the siege, a provisional national assembly was formed by socialist and left-wing republicans who vowed to continue the fight against the enemy. They set up the "Paris Commune," in emulation of the radical Jacobin Assembly of 1793, and in defiance of the right-wing National Assembly that had convened at Versailles to conclude a peace treaty, ceding Alsace and Lorraine to Germany. This revolutionary socialist movement was brutally crushed by the Versailles troops in May 1871, with tens of thousands of casualties.

The Two World Wars
German expansionism would lead directly to the two "world" wars of the twentieth century. Both were fought partly on French soil, and you can visit some of the sites of First World War trench warfare in the northeast of France, and also the beaches of Normandy, where Allied troops landed in 1944 to wrest back Western Europe from Hitler.

France was a central pillar of the alliance against Germany in the First World War, and suffered greatly. A quarter of all French men between the ages of eighteen and twenty-seven were killed—1.25 million men—and another 4 million were wounded. By the terms of the peace treaty imposed upon Germany in 1919, in the same Hall of Mirrors at Versailles, Alsace and Lorraine were returned to France.

The Second World War produced another of France's "strong leaders," this time in the person of General Charles de Gaulle, who led the Free French government in exile in London and headed the French resistance movement, or *maquis*. The Third Republic had lasted until Nazi Germany's invasion of France in 1940. The southern half of the country was then governed by a collaborationist regime in Vichy under Marshal Pétain until 1942, when the Germans occupied all of France. De Gaulle, who refused to accept the truce of 1940, broadcast to the nation to continue the struggle. The resistance movement waged a guerrilla war against the German occupation, and the Free French troops fought with the Allied forces. The scars of the war years continue to be felt in France today.

Decolonization

In the chaotic years following the Second World War, France's Fourth Republic was marked by rapid changes of government and political instability, and by colonial insurrection. The colonies of Indochina—Laos, Cambodia, and Vietnam—that had been liberated from the Japanese and handed back to France embarked on

struggles for independence (1946–54). No sooner
was this over than the Algerian War of
Independence broke out (1954–62). Algeria had
an Arab population, a Berber population, and a
large population of French settlers. For the
French, colonization had always been a process of
absorbing its overseas territories into French life
as fully as possible—French language, culture,
hierarchy, and lifestyle. In 1954 the
Algerians revolted against this
imposition and the resulting savage
war disrupted both Algerian and,
increasingly, French life. As a result
the government fell, and in 1958
France called upon its wartime
leader Charles de Gaulle to
become prime minister.

De Gaulle proclaimed the Fifth
Republic, with himself as its first
president, in 1959, consolidating
executive power in presidential
hands. To the fury of the French
settlers, he declared that Algeria should become
a self-governing, independent country. Many of
these colonists returned to France, mainly to
the south, and were known as *pieds noirs*
("black feet"), and increasing numbers of
Algerians also migrated to France to work in
its factories.

The Algerian war started a chain reaction by the end of which, in 1959–60, virtually all of France's former colonial possessions were granted independence. Algeria itself gained independence in 1962.

General de Gaulle retired from office in 1969 and died in 1970. His successor Georges Pompidou is best remembered for his interest in architecture. The Pompidou Center in Paris is a leading arts complex. After Georges Pompidou died in office, Valéry Giscard d'Estaing was elected president (1974–81), followed by the Socialist François Mitterand, who served two terms (1981–94), before dying of cancer in 1996. He was succeeded in 1995 by his prime minister, Jacques Chirac, who fought off a challenge from the ultra-right National Front party leader, Jean Marie Le Pen, to win a second five-year term in 2002.

On July 14, 1989, France celebrated the bicentenary of the Republic with a six-hundred-mile picnic on a line of identically colored patterned tablecloths covering the country from north to south.

France today is a patchwork of nationalities, with significant numbers of immigrants from southern Europe, North Africa, and Vietnam. There are approximately two-and-a-half million immigrants—who form a small but noticeable part of the total population.

GOVERNMENT

Charles de Gaulle once said, "The French will only be united under the threat of danger. Nobody can simply bring together a country that has 265 kinds of cheese."

France is a multiparty republic. The head of government is the prime minister, and the head of state is the president. The president is elected for five years by direct universal suffrage. He appoints the prime minister and, on the prime minister's recommendation, the other members of the government. He presides over the Council of Ministers, promulgates Acts of Parliament, is commander in chief of the armed forces, and can dissolve the National Assembly and exercise emergency powers in a crisis.

The prime minister sets national policy and carries it out under the direction of the president. The prime minister, as head of government, implements legislation.

This can give rise to the uncomfortable situation, as happened between center-right President Chirac and his socialist prime minister, Lionel Jospin, where president and prime minister are at political odds with one another.

The French Parliament (*Parlement*) has two houses. The upper house is the Senate (*Sénat*), and consists of 321 members elected by indirect universal suffrage for a nine-year term. One-third

is reelected every three years. The National
Assembly has 577 members, and is elected on
direct universal suffrage for five years. Both
houses are responsible for drawing up and passing
legislation. In the case of disagreement, the
National Assembly makes the final decision.

There are six main parties or coalitions
represented in the National Assembly.

Partie Socialiste (PS) (Socialist Party)

Rassemblement Pour la République (RPR)
(Rally for the Republic)

Union pour la Démocratie Française et du Centre (UDF)
(Union for French Democracy)

Démocratie Libérale et Indépendantes (DL) (Liberal Democrats)

Groupe Communiste (PCF) (Communist Party)

Radical, Citoyen et Vert (RCV) (Green Party)

France, as we have seen, is governed according
to a national civil legal system—the *Code
Napoléon*. One impact of the code is on contracts,
which are often shorter than British or American
ones, where the French simply refer to a clause in
the *Code Napoléon*.

The final part of France's governmental
system is the judiciary. The highest court of
appeal is the *Conseil d'État*, which judges the
legality of constitutional and administrative acts

and advises the government on draft legislation. The highest judicial court is the *Cour de Cassation*, which can set aside or quash judgments and remit cases for rehearing to the thirty-five courts of appeal for retrial.

THE EUROZONE

France is a full member of NATO, and was a founding member of the European Economic Community in 1956, an ideal promoted by a Frenchman, Jean Monnet. The European Union came into being under the leadership of another Frenchman, Jacques Delors, and the European Parliament is based in the French city of Strasbourg. European Union laws and directives are debated in the French *Parlement* and incorporated into French law and practice. On January 1, 1999, the Euro became a fully fledged currency and on January 1, 2002, the Euro replaced the franc as France's currency.

FRANCE AND THE UNITED STATES

The French tend to lump the British and the Americans together under one term, "*les Anglo-Saxons*," underestimating the multiracial nature of both the United States and, increasingly, Great Britain. However, France has an enduring affection for the United States, shown by French support for the American Revolution and America's support for France in the World Wars and subsequently. France benefited from American financial support after World War II, and has also benefited from American artists' and writers' love affairs with French culture from the 1920s through to the present day. For example, at the great Impressionist artist Claude Monet's house in Giverny, in Normandy, there is a permanent exhibition of the work of American Impressionists.

Many American veterans and their families make yearly pilgrimages to visit the cemeteries near Caen, and the beaches of Normandy where American, British, Canadian, Commonwealth, and French forces landed on June 6, 1944, in "Operation Overlord" to liberate Western Europe from German occupation.

Incidentally, some U.S. statesmen have had strong connections with France. Before the Revolution, Benjamin Franklin was sent by Congress to Paris to negotiate a treaty in 1776. After negotiating both a commercial treaty and a defensive alliance, he was appointed sole plenipotentiary to France in 1778 and stayed there until 1785. Thomas Jefferson was the U.S.

minister to France from 1785 to 1789. And, of course, John F. Kennedy's wife was born Jacqueline Bouvier, of French descent.

This affection has been only slightly dented by the invasion of American English in the IT and music industries, and by the incursion of McDonald's on the French food scene. More serious perhaps, is the French concern about the danger of globalization led by American corporations, and the recent difficulties of the one great French international corporation, Vivendi Universal, may have served only to emphasize this.

What are the French like? What do they believe in, and what principles do they live by? This is the subject of the next chapter.

VALUES & ATTITUDES

France is different. Everyone agrees. Not everyone agrees what the differences are, but no one doubts that they exist. The saying "*L'exception Française*," "the French exception," means that, whatever the general rules, France plays by her own rules and protects her own interests first of all, and that French things are best done by or through French people.

CHANGING THE RULES OF THE GAME— A "WHY" CULTURE

Within limits, other European countries accept situations as they stand and ask how best to achieve a given result. The French ask why the result should be achieved in the first place. This questioning and argumentative spirit usually sends everybody back to the drawing board and sets schedules back by hours, days, or weeks. It is one of the reasons why "expletive deleted" often accompanies the word "French" in other European countries as people express their frustration with French intransigence.

THE IDEAS SOCIETY

Part of the readiness to question comes from French education itself. In France, intellectualism is not a dirty word. French children in the upper secondary schools all study philosophy as part of the school curriculum. They are taught to think logically and to debate. The French are more tolerant of impracticability than of inconsistency. In any discussion, they will depart from a central statement and proceed logically to a conclusion. They will criticize you for your faulty logic, rather than for your impractical solutions, and they will be stubborn in holding to their own ideas unless you can find some way of demonstrating that their logic is wrong or that there is an alternative logical solution.

René Descartes (1596–1650), the French philosopher and mathematician, is known as "the father of modern philosophy." He codified the French system of logical thinking—Cartesian logic. His most famous dictum is, "I think, therefore I am."

In France it is important to be *sérieux* (this is a necessary quality in a French *cadre*, or senior manager, for example). Therefore education, intelligence, and eloquence are prized.

Sérieux also means professional. A French term of criticism is "*Ce n'est pas sérieux*" ("It's a joke—not professional"). So if a French person accuses you of not being serious, it means that you are not behaving professionally, rather than that you do not mean what you say.

This abstract thinking and love of rational order shows in the ordering of nature in the famous formal gardens laid out by Le Nôtre at Versailles and the Louvre in the seventeenth century. However, it would be a mistake to confuse the French love of rationalism with a desire for clear, straightforward, practical systems.

The French live happily with apparent contradictions. They see nothing incongruous in keeping old-fashioned plumbing in the bathroom and installing the most up-to-date gadgetry in the kitchen. Or in driving a long distance to enjoy a two-hour lunch, combining a passion for the open countryside with a tolerance of cramped, dark living spaces, permitting dogs (sometimes on velvet cushions) in restaurants where children aren't allowed, or using expensive perfume but not bothering with deodorant.

FRENCH STYLE

The French combine logic with wit, flair, and elegance. They enjoy plays on words, rhetoric, and satire rather than practical jokes or "belly laughs," and if you watch a talk show on French TV you will be impressed by the speed of reaction and by the witty observations made by contributors. Humor in business meetings is, on the whole, not expected.

For the French, style and flair in presentation, including self-presentation, is important. The French hate being bored. They enjoy a good argument, and will take the other side just for the hell of it. They need to feel intellectual validity in everything they do, and if their attention is not engaged they will actively show they are distracted, begin mini-conversations, talk on their cellphones, or get up and leave a meeting.

The preeminent manifestation of French style is food and fashion. Haute couture and its attendants, perfume, make-up, and accessories are not just a major industry but have iconic status. In France it is important, especially for women, to be properly coiffed and properly dressed, and you will find, if you live or work regularly in France, that you will be affected by this.

BEING FRENCH

The French are often criticized for being chauvinistic and distrustful of other nations. On a practical level this is merely self-interest, but for France the very concept of Frenchness and *la Francophonie* (the French-speaking world) is important.

This does not mean that France is closed to outside influences. On the contrary, France has eagerly imported novelty from all over the world. It's just that when something has been imported, it becomes—well, French.

To preserve the concept of Frenchness, France will invest in prestigious projects that also have practical benefits, both for the image of France and for French business. These may vary from nuclear explosions in the Pacific, in the face of international criticism, to the success of the Airbus, or the architectural marvels of the Louvre or the Beaubourg in Paris, or indeed the speed of France's TGV (*Train à grande vitesse*—high-speed train).

A key part of being French is respect for the French language. In school it is important to learn to speak French properly, and especially to write it. Written French is much more formal than its equivalent in the U.S.A. or the U.K., with a focus on correct grammar, spelling, and punctuation rather than on free expression.

It's important to remember that French was the language of diplomacy and of educated people from the sixteenth to the early twentieth centuries. In 1635 Cardinal Richelieu, Louis XIII's chief minister, founded the Académie Française, with the brief of working "with all care and diligence to give certain rules to our language, and to render it pure, eloquent, and capable of treating the arts and sciences." At the same time regional dialects or languages (called *patois*) were banned, and children would be beaten at school for speaking them—a practice that continued in France's colonial territories.

The principle of purification continues today. The Académie Française remains responsible for the protection of the language, and regularly fights a rearguard action against the horrors of imported words, especially in the IT, food and drink, and media industries. "Franglais" may be alive and well in the city streets, and *argot*, or slang, has a part to play, but there is still a concern with correct thought and expression.

According to the 1994 *Loi Toubon* (after minister of culture, Jacques Toubon), all product descriptions, labels, advertisements, instructions, and signs must be in French. Trademarks are exempt from this law. The British cosmetics company Body Shop has been fined for having English labels on its products. Radio stations are fined if they don't play 40 percent French music. Films on French TV must be 60 percent European-made, of which 40 percent must be French.

Language is not only an ideological weapon in France's armory of "Frenchness." It is also the subject of genuinely popular interest. When the French government proposed banning the "g" in *oignon* (onion), people petitioned in protest, as they did in the War of the Circumflex, the speech mark over a vowel in some words, such as *maître* (master), *huître* (oyster), and *forêt* (forest), that often denotes a missing "s" but has little or no effect on pronunciation. Language games on TV are as popular as soap operas. Seven million people watch *La Grande Dictée*, a spelling competition that attracts 300,000 entrants.

The result of all this is that the French will not necessarily applaud you for your halting French. They would expect you to speak their language well. If you are not at least reasonably confident, you are probably better speaking clearly in English—and apologizing for not being able to speak French.

The French love of language extends to literature. The French read widely, and the traditional divide between politics and the arts is much less pronounced than in other countries. André Malraux, writer, wartime resistance leader, and politician, was a  prime example, as were Lamartine, De Tocqueville, and Châteaubriand in the nineteenth century.

President Jacques Chirac has described poetry as "a necessity for daily living."

The other linchpin of being French is French culture. With some reason, the French believe they have made a preeminent claim to world culture in art, music, painting, and thought. They are, if you will believe them, and many do, the premier civilized culture in the world.

There is still considerable French government investment in the spread of French language and culture through the Alliance Française and French cultural missions overseas. Above all, there is the concept of *La Francophonie* (a concept supported by a government organization, linking the common interests of all countries where French is spoken). It's a concept similar in principle to, but much tighter in practice than, the British Commonwealth of former colonies.

FAMILY FIRST

French families, traditionally, are highly integrated. Children often live with their parents until they marry, and an entire family of three or four generations may live in the same household. If they don't, the family members will tend to live reasonably close to each other and will meet regularly for Sunday lunch or on festivals. Because the family is the first source of business resources or partners in new ventures, the focus of discussion will be about business as well as pleasure.

The French family is also very private. You'll read more about this in "The French at Home," in Chapter 4. Only the most intimate friends are brought into family gatherings, and to be invited is a great honor.

The importance of the family at the local level is replicated at the national level. France likes to think of herself as a national family, bound together under the French flag by French experience and, above all, by the French language.

At the same time—remember the ability to live with inconsistency—the French feel that the security of the family is no bar to sexual license. Marital fidelity isn't expected. The French are mildly amused at the American and British media uproar about which politician is found in bed with which man or woman. When French President François Mitterand died in 1996, his wife and his daughter were at his graveside, and so were his mistress and her daughter by the former president. The early evening "happy hour" in U.S. and British wine bars and pubs often has a different connotation in France, being the time when most affairs are conducted! What the "Anglo-Saxons" see as licentiousness, the French regard as just another aspect of life. What they object to is the intrusion of the media.

Although France is primarily a Catholic country, illegitimacy carries no stigma (except among strict Catholics), and "living in sin" (unmarried couples living together) is not a problem.

What everyone is concerned about is discretion, so that the dignity and integrity of the family are preserved.

BEHAVING CORRECTLY

We've mentioned the expression, "*Ce n'est pas sérieux*" ("It's unprofessional"). Now here's another one: "*Ce n'est pas correcte*" ("It's not the right way to behave"). In France, etiquette is important. For example, you don't say just "*Bonjour.*" You say "*Bonjour, Monsieur*" or "*Bonjour, Madame.*" Adding the "Sir" or "Madam" is correct behavior. Omitting it is incorrect, even vulgar.

The French set great store by correct behavior, and the sooner you learn the rules the better. Unfortunately the American "Have a nice day" familiarity is not considered correct behavior. The French tend to consider American dress and manners careless, naïve, and unsophisticated, and to mock the British for dressing badly and having no sense of *savoir faire* (how to behave in polite society).

For the French, behaving correctly doesn't necessarily mean smiling and being polite. It can mean showing cool indifference, not admitting when you are wrong, and, above all, understanding the many social snobbisms that still exist in French society.

The French Revolution did not create complete equality, either of birth or of opportunity. What it did was to replace the power of the monarch and the aristocracy with the power of the *bourgeoisie*, which was exactly the original intention.

In today's France the *haute bourgeoisie*, the upper middle class, is as much a caste as its aristocratic predecessors, leading the country in both business and government, attending the top universities and training schools, and gravitating between government and leading businesses. To be Daddy's little boy or, to an increasing extent, little girl, still eases your path into the higher echelons of business or politics.

The *bonne bourgeoisie*, or professional middle classes, are the young people from "good" families who are rising in business and politics. Nicknamed "*bon chic bons gens*," or "BCBG," these are the ones who will rise quickly by behaving correctly.

The *petite bourgeoisie* are the trading classes, the grocers. These are often kept at a social distance, and one reason may be that there is a closer relationship between the traders and manual and factory workers. A traditional example in the village might have been a farm worker "marrying up" by marrying the local primary school teacher. But there is a feeling generally that one should keep to one's own group.

chapter three

CUSTOM & TRADITION

Despite its tradition of central and unitary government, France has retained a strong regional culture, with great variations in food, wine, sport, and ways of living. Many of the French people you meet will identify more with their native region, such as Brittany, Alsace, or Provence, than with the national French culture typified by Paris. France has the highest proportion of second homes in the world, and most of these belong to people who live and work in or near Paris but whose family roots are in the provinces.

It is important to note that there has been a significant move to decentralize governmental functions throughout the provinces. The very efficient French telecommunications and transport infrastructure has made it much easier to run successful businesses in the provinces than used to be the case.

Regional languages are still spoken in parts of France—Breton in Brittany, Flemish in the northeast, German in Alsace, Spanish dialects in the southwest, and Italian in Corsica. Some 21 percent of French people claim to speak a regional language well, and 14 percent fairly well.

CHURCH AND STATE

France has no official religion, but is over 90 percent Catholic, so the French observe both religious and secular holidays. In France, Church and state are officially separate, and the Catholic Church receives no direct funding from the government. The Church runs a large number of private schools, however, that are partly state funded. Only 2 percent of the French population is Protestant, but France has one of the largest Jewish populations in Europe—about 700,000 (mainly from North Africa)—and over a million Muslims.

The key word in describing relations between Church and state in France is *laïcité*. It signifies that France is neutral in matters of belief and refuses to give any belief priority. However, for all practical purposes, France is a Catholic country. In the past, when Catholicism was the official religion of the French monarchy, France was considered "the eldest daughter of the Church." Napoleon concluded a concordat with Pope Pius VII in Rome in 1801, regulating relations with the papacy. This lasted until 1905, when Church and state were legally separated. In Alsace and Lorraine, regions that were part of Germany in 1905, the concordat is still law. Strasbourg University, in Alsace, is the only university with a department of theology that has separate corridors for the Catholic and Protestant sections. Alsace is the only *département* that pays rabbis, pastors, and priests salaries equal to teachers'. The teaching of religion in France is forbidden in state schools, and there is concern about outward displays of religion.

Nevertheless the Catholic liturgy deeply affects daily life and, of course, festivals. In the Catholic liturgy each day is dedicated to a saint of the Catholic Church, whose name you may bear. So on your name day you might choose to take the day off. Your village or town will be dedicated to a saint, and the saint's day may be a reason for a holiday. This is, after all, a country where the name of the saint's day accompanies the weather forecast on TV. And on the feast of St. Jacques (St. James) the announcer will greet you with "*Bonne Fête Saint Jacques.*"

Even with a predominantly Catholic population, church attendance is falling to around 10 percent of the population in Paris and 15 percent elsewhere, with attendance lowest in the eighteen-to-thirty-five age group. In most places in France, however, you will find a church congregation with the mass in French, sometimes in English, and even in Latin. To find out about religious services for your denomination, contact the local town hall (*Mairie*), information office (*Syndicat d'Initiative*), or *Office de Tourisme* in the south. You can also find out about churches and church services in the Yellow Pages (*Pages Jaunes*) or on the Internet under *Églises* (churches) or *Cultes* (religious centers).

What is interesting is that, despite the fall in church attendance, families still baptize their babies in church, and celebrate First Communion for twelve-year-olds, and weddings. These are big social occasions for the family and relatives, and are seen as part of a good upbringing and socializing as much as an expression of religious belief.

Islam plays an increasingly important part in French life. About a million Muslims live in France, mainly from North Africa, and although there are no nationally recognized Islamic festivals, the period of Ramadan and the festivals of Id el Fitr and Id el Kebir are important ceremonies in French Islamic life.

HOLIDAYS

France respects hard work, but not workaholics. "Work hard but enjoy life," is the watchword. Officially, the French work a thirty-five-hour week. In fact, they work more than this, but have more national holidays and regional holidays than the United States or the United Kingdom. They also have a longer holiday entitlement of five weeks a year.

THE NATIONAL HOLIDAYS OF FRANCE

Date	English Name	French Name
January 1	New Year's Day	*Jour de l'An*
March/April	Easter Sunday/ Easter Monday	*Pâques*
May 1	Labor Day	*Fête du Travail*
May 8	Victory in Europe Day	*Fête de la Libération*
Early May (40 days after Easter)	Ascension	*Ascension*
Late May	Whit Sunday/ Whit Monday	*Pentecôte*
July 14	Bastille Day	*Fête Nationale*
August 15	Assumption of the Virgin Mary	*L'Assomption de la Sainte Marie*
November 1	All Saints' Day	*Toussaint*
November 11	Remembrance Day	*Armistice 1918*
December 25	Christmas Day	*Noel*

If a holiday falls on a Thursday or a Tuesday, the French will "make the bridge" (*faire le pont*) and take a long weekend by including the intervening Friday or Monday as well.

THE FESTIVE YEAR

Christmas

The festivities start on Christmas Eve, when families decorate their trees and, if they are Catholics, go to midnight mass. This is called "Joseph, Mary and the angels" (*Joseph, Marie et les Anges*). Returning home, they celebrate the *réveillon*, a large late supper of traditional foods. These will vary by region and may include *foie gras* (goose or duck liver preserved in its own fat), *huîtres* (oysters), or buckwheat pancakes and seafood in Brittany. In Alsace you may eat goose, and in Provence, fish. Also in Provence, traditional homes may serve thirteen kinds of dessert, named for different religious orders—Augustines, Bénédictines, Franciscans, and so on. These are various pastries and concoctions of dried fruits.

A typical meal might be a starter of oysters (which are at their best at this time of year), followed by *charcuterie* (cold meats), which might include *foie gras*. The main course is goose, capon, or turkey, served with chestnuts, followed by salad, a choice of cheeses, and a cake shaped like a log. Presents are usually exchanged on Christmas Eve, or, according to family tradition, on Christmas Day or even New Year's Day. They are opened around the Christmas tree or Nativity scene, often while listening to Christmas carols.

Père Noel is the name for Father Christmas. The greeting on Christmas day is "*Joyeux Noel*," or "Happy Christmas," and the reply is the same. In Catholic families the Nativity scene is set up in stages between Christmas Eve and January 6, the Epiphany, or Three Kings (*les Rois Mages*), when the images of the three kings are added to complete the scene.

As in many other Catholic countries, Christmas is the time for the Christmas crib to be set up in the main square and for nativity plays to be presented.

New Year

New Year is a special time for the French, with celebrations the night before, and a huge family meal with friends invited, often featuring turkey and chestnuts, on New Year's Day. To greet people in the New Year, say "*Bonne Année*," and expect the same in response.

The patron saint of the New Year is St. Sylvester, and the New Year is sometimes called *St. Sylvestre* in his honor. In the center of Paris traffic is banned for the night and the streets are filled with people. It is a wonderful sight with all the decorations lit up and monuments floodlit, but don't expect to find a cab home unless you have prebooked one.

Twelfth Night

As in many Catholic countries, Twelfth Night assumes a special importance as it commemorates the three kings bringing gifts to the infant Jesus. Although it is not a public holiday, in many places a special cake, called "*la galette des Rois*," is baked with a bean, a coin, or an almond inside. Whoever finds the bean, coin, or almond is crowned King or Queen for the day.

In addition to the festivals listed here there are many local festivals, and information about these can be found at the local *Syndicat d'Initiative* or *Office de Tourisme.*

Easter

Easter is the next major public holiday, falling in March or April and celebrated according to the Catholic fashion. On Good Friday, two days before Easter Sunday, many shops will be closed to commemorate the crucifixion of Christ, but on Saturday the shops reopen and people stock up for the Easter Sunday and Easter Monday celebrations. Easter Sunday is one of the great church-going days of the year, followed by the traditional gastronomic blowout, and Easter Monday is a traditional time for sporting activity.

Before Easter there may be local festivals celebrating Shrove Tuesday and Ash Wednesday, the beginning of Lent, the six-week period of purification and fasting. Palm Sunday, one week before Easter Sunday, celebrates the entry of Christ into Jerusalem. These may be occasions for special church services, but are not holidays. At Easter itself, you may hear people wishing you "*Joyeuses Pâques*" ("Happy Easter"), and you should say the same.

May 1 and May 8

May 1 is Labor Day, celebrated by local parades, and a few days later Victory in Europe Day celebrates the liberation of Europe from the Nazis in 1945. This is particularly important in France, which was partially occupied by Germany from 1940 to 1945. Memorial services are held, and there are parades of *anciens combatants* (war veterans), all with their campaign ribbons and standards, in city centers, around the town halls, and at services in the cemeteries.

Ascension Day and Pentecost

Forty days after Easter, Ascension Day marks the ascension of the risen Christ into heaven to take his place at the right hand of God. Once again this is a religious festival with church services and processions. Similar celebrations take place on the

Sunday and Monday of *Pentecôte*, which commemorates the Holy Spirit's gift of tongues to the twelve apostles of Christ, enabling them to go out and preach his message.

July 14
This national celebration commemorates the 1789 storming of the Bastille prison in Paris, the effective start of the French Revolution. This is a secular festival, marked by parades and much playing of the French national anthem, *La Marseillaise*, with fireworks and dancing in the streets till morning.

The Assumption and All Saints
Two more religious festivals follow. The Assumption, on August 15 *(L'Assomption de la Sainte Marie)*, celebrates the ascent of the Virgin Mary, mother of Christ, into heaven. This is a big celebration, when families gather together.

All Saints, on November 1, commemorates the dead, and is the time when families visit the graves of their departed and lay flowers (often chrysanthemums) there.

Halloween, very popular with children in America and increasingly in Britain, passes almost unnoticed in France, perhaps because of the country's predominantly Catholic persuasion. However, it has a following in parts of Paris where there is an American college and a large expatriate population of American and British citizens.

Remembrance Day
Armistice Day on November 11 commemorates the end of the First World War, in which France lost 1.25 million people. This is a solemn day of remembrance of all those who died in the wars in which France was involved in the twentieth century. It is marked in Paris by the President and senior officials laying wreaths at the tomb of the Unknown Soldier at the foot of the Arc de Triomphe, and by similar ceremonies and processions at war memorials throughout France.

And finally, back to Christmas, with all the "Anglo-Saxon" razzamatazz, and with the continuing debates about whether commercialism is smothering Christmas or keeping it alive.

Apart from the formal set-piece celebrations, France offers a huge variety of local celebrations, and you can find out about these from the local *Office de Tourisme* or *Syndicat d'Initiative*. There are many customs and traditions that people all over France take as a matter of course, and in which you, as a visitor, will be welcome to participate.

chapter four

MAKING FRIENDS

The French have a reputation for being cold, arrogant, pushy, and rude. This is not, of course, the case, but they do have social standards that can pose problems for both casual tourists and new residents. Although some visitors assume that as they are guests in France, the French should take the initiative in welcoming them, it's the guest's job to adapt and fit in. Once the French recognize that you have made the effort, you will be fully accepted—possibly rather more than you want!

French children are still brought up to be polite to their elders, and to preserve a certain degree of formality. American children are brought up to express themselves, and politeness often goes by the board. These are both clichés, but one of the first things for a visitor to France to learn is the necessity for politeness at all times. For the French it is important to be correct, and they will be looking for good manners from you too. Even the French Hell's Angels have their etiquette.

The Cool Stare

Many American and British people are used to acknowledging passing strangers with a smile or a nod. The French see no reason to do so, and foreigners in France find this unnerving; but don't be put off. Polly Platt, in her book *French or Foe?*, describes this well. It's not impoliteness, it's just French style. To smile for no reason is not *sérieux*. A French person may smile at a stranger during a *moment de complicité*, a moment of shared pleasure at an unusual or amusing incident observed by both. The French smile a lot when they feel there is something to smile about; otherwise they remain deadpan. There is a story (variously told about Presidents Mitterand and Chirac) that, when shown a photo of their president smiling, the French simply failed to recognize him!

GETTING TO MEET EXPATRIATES

The big cities of France, especially Paris, are truly international communities, and all foreigners have one thing in common: the need to learn French. One of the best ways to meet other foreigners is in French classes (see page 80, below).

Paris has been home to foreign expatriates for centuries, and expatriate organizations are well developed and a mine of information and support to new arrivals. A selected list of organizations is in the Resources section at the end of this book.

One organization, based outside Paris, is the Acceuil des Villes Françaises. Its aim is to provide centers in which newcomers, both French and foreign, can meet each other, and has six hundred branches in cities throughout the country. The local group is called by the name of the town, for example Nice Acceuil, and you can find the address of your local branch from the town hall (*Mairie*). Membership is by annual subscription (low) and activities vary from town to town, but may include art, cookery classes, sports, and group travel. To find your nearest Acceuil group, look in the Yellow Pages under *Associations, organismes culturels et socio-educatifs*, the *Bottin Téléphonique*, or the magazine *Pariscope*.

GETTING TO MEET THE FRENCH

Common interests are a good way to meet people. Find a group that pursues your special interest, and join it. One way to make friends in the countryside is to join the local ramblers. The *randonnée* is a French institution, leading walks or bicycle rides *en masse* with an organized itinerary. You find out what's on and where, probably from the *Mairie* notice board, turn up, pay a small fee, collect a map, and set off along the path in small groups. There are lunch and snack breaks, and the opportunity to meet and talk to people, and to practice your French.

L'Amitié

Friendship is not taken lightly in France. When a French family takes you to its heart there is a covert but strongly felt range of mutual responsibilities and duties to be undertaken. You will be asked, and expected, to go to dinner, have lunch, go to the beach, join them for *apéritifs* and cocktails, and spend time talking to them on the telephone. Should you need to excuse yourself—because you're washing your hair, have a headache, or simply have a previous appointment—you may have the feeling that you are letting your friends down.

Judy Churchill, a trainer and consultant in the south of France, says that friendship needs working at. French people expect reciprocity in relationships. They can be very warm at first, but can withdraw in disappointment if they are not responded to in kind. Many stories are told of southern French people extending the hand of friendship to foreign visitors, only to feel let down after they have left and the contact is not kept up.

INVITATIONS HOME

French social life can be very easygoing, but it can also be quite structured. After years of being *bien élevés*, French people are quick to spot any examples of bad manners or social uncouthness. Much of the protocol surrounds food and hospitality.

The first thing to remember is that food is of paramount interest in French society: the appreciation of food, its aesthetic qualities, its presentation, taste and, above all, the surroundings in which it is served.

In big cities most people invite guests to restaurants, partly for reasons of space, partly for reasons of time, and invitations to a private house are infrequent. Outside the cities the home is much more a place for entertainment, but the pressure of producing and hosting a big meal means that people are unwilling to invite you to their house unless they can get things exactly right. The "drop-in" culture is uncommon in France. But in the south of France, because of the climate, open house is much more common.

So what is the alternative? It's the *apéritif*. People often invite you for an *apéro* or *apéritif* to give them a chance to get to know you for an hour or two over a drink. An *apéro* might take place at lunch time or early evening, and is reasonably informal. You'll notice on arrival that you are invited into the main room, but are unlikely to be shown around the house or into the kitchen. The French like to keep their houses private, so don't expect a "grand tour." You certainly shouldn't go into the kitchen uninvited. One French colleague said that for twenty-five years he never entered his grandmother's kitchen until she became too arthritic to carry dishes for herself and had to ask for help.

Sunday lunch is the big occasion. If you are invited for noon or 1 p.m., don't plan anything else for the rest of the day. Lunch is served in a relaxed, leisurely fashion, followed by a nap or a walk, or perhaps both, and the whole occasion can easily stretch out over five or six hours.

In many French families, children are still taught to ask permission to leave the table after a meal. In the last ten years the attitude toward children has become much more relaxed and understanding, especially in the expression of emotion. If a child jumps up excitedly from the table before the meal is over the adults do not necessarily say "*Ne bouges pas de table, s'il te plait*" ("Don't move from the table, please"), as they would have a few years ago.

Timing

The French themselves are not precise about timing. You should not arrive on time; ten to fifteen minutes late is acceptable. French people will expect to arrive about half an hour late.

Gift Giving

If you're invited into a French house you should always take a small gift—flowers, a plant, or chocolates.

If you take flowers they should be odd numbers (seven is fine, but never thirteen) and be sure to unwrap them before presenting them. Once again, different flowers have different connotations. Do not give carnations, which mean bad luck to some people, or chrysanthemums, which are the flowers placed on the graves of loved ones at *Toussaint* (All Saints), and signify death. Roses signify love or socialist politics. Yellow roses are associated with cuckoldry, as is the color yellow in general.

The French are an artistic nation. They will appreciate a book, a CD, or a picture that appeals to their aesthetic sense.

The French culinary and wine tradition means that items of foreign food and drink are not necessarily well received—unless it's something like Scotch whiskey. Do not take wine unless it is very special, and, of course, is French.

Bon Appétit

Mealtimes have their own protocol. The French equivalent of "Enjoy!" at the beginning of a meal is "*Bon appétit,*" and you should respond with the same words. Don't taste wine until your host has raised his or her glass and said, "*À votre santé*" ("To your health!"), and you should reply in the same way and clink glasses.

As a rule of thumb, faced with an arrangement of knives, forks, and spoons, you should start at the outside and work inward. Usually you will find a smaller fork and a bigger fork on the left, and a little knife and a big knife on the right. You may be expected to keep your knife and fork for the next course. See what others are doing. Naturally, this would not be the case if you started with fish, and meat were to follow—the fish knife and fork would be removed. The dessert spoon and the coffee spoon will often be at the top, parallel to you, one facing one way and one facing the other.

French tables will usually have three glasses: one for water (the largest), one for red wine, and one for white wine (the smallest). Water is not normally served first.

The Order of the Meal
In France, salad is served after the main dish, and cheese precedes dessert. The cheese course can be a hazard. Help yourself from the cheese dish only once, to up to three different cheeses, and cut them in such a way as to preserve the shape of what is left (that is, don't cut the point off).

Knives, Forks, and Fingers
It is rude to point your knife at people to emphasize what you are saying. Do not pick up any food with your fingers except bread, which you should always break with your fingers, never cut with a knife. Eat your piece of bread, and take another. The French will eat bread all through the meal, but do not use it to wipe their plates. Eat everything on your plate. The French consider Americans wasteful as they often leave food.

Drinking
Don't get drunk. French people alternate wine with water, and sip their wines so that the drinking doesn't get in the way of the conversation. Also, do not help yourself to wine, unless you are invited to.

Smoking

In cafés and bars the French smoke continuously, but in a restaurant or at someone's house wait until the end of the meal, when the *digestif* is served. Don't smoke between courses. If you're not sure if smoking is acceptable, ask.

Walking About

Don't wander into the private areas of a house or apartment. These include the kitchen and also the bathroom. On the whole, French people will not expect to use the bathroom while at dinner, and your hosts may not have prepared the room for use by visitors.

It is *correcte* to send a written "thank you" note after receiving hospitality or a gift, rather than simply to make a phone call.

SOCIAL CUSTOMS

There are small social things that the French do in everyday life without thinking, but that the foreigner needs to learn in order not stick out like a sore and rather vulgar thumb. For the French it is important to be *correcte*, and they notice immediately if someone steps out of line. Etiquette, or *estique*, was invented by the French. *Estique* meant daily rules for soldiers, but came to mean etiquette, rules of social behavior for entry into polite society. The French *Bottin Mondain* (a register of the social elite in France) contains a list of etiquette rules as long as your arm—a sort of Emily Post of French manners—but certain guidelines are useful for any social occasion.

Formality in Greetings

The French are far more formal than you might expect. If you address someone it should be "*Bonjour, Monsieur*" or "*Bonjour, Madame,*" never just "*Bonjour.*" In a small shop, or in a hotel breakfast room, people may say "*Bonjour, Messieurs Dames*" on entering, and "*Au revoir, Messieurs Dames*" on leaving. It is very common on completing a transaction in a shop to say "*Bonne journée*" ("Have a good day") or "*Bonne soirée*" ("Have a good evening"). The standard reply is "*Merci*" or "*Je vous remercie*" ("Thank you"). If you meet somebody with a title, it is important to use it. A retired ambassador is *Monsieur l'Ambassadeur*; the head of a company is *Monsieur le Président* or *Madame la Présidente*.

It is important to say "*s'il vous plaît*" and "*merci.*" It is important not to interrupt strangers unless you say "*Excusez-moi de vous déranger*" ("Excuse me for interrupting you") and to add to it, "*j'ai un petit problème*" ("I have a small problem") and to ask, "*Est-ce-que vous pourriez m'aider?*" ("Could you help me?") to get cooperation and support.

Le Shake-hand

French people shake hands on arriving and leaving, even at work. If you meet a friend in a café and he or she is with a group of people, it is normal to shake hands with everybody in the group. You will find people shaking hands with others in the group while continuing to talk to the person they are greeting. The reason for shaking hands, traditionally, was to prove that you weren't holding a dagger.

The Kiss

Many French women and men kiss on the cheek on first meeting. Take your cue from the person you are greeting as to whether to kiss or shake hands, but it's never just one kiss on one cheek. Usually it's two in Paris, three in the provinces, and four in the south, and among the young and family members.

Tutoyer

If you speak French you will know that there is a difference between the formal pronoun *vous* (you) and the informal singular *tu*. Never use the informal *tu* unless you are invited to. It is a serious social offense of overfamiliarity. Whereas in the English-speaking world formality is seen to be a distancing factor in a relationship, in France *vous* is the norm until familiarity allows otherwise. The exception is with children, and among teenagers and students, who use *tu* to each other with impunity. As David Hampshire puts it, "The familiar form is always used with children, animals and God, but almost never with your elders or work superiors."

Dress

One used to be able to tell when an English girl in Paris had acquired a French boyfriend by how she suddenly smartened up, changed her hairstyle, and began using lipstick. That may have changed, but the importance of dress has not. For men, dark suits, bright ties, and a good aftershave are *de rigueur*. For women, however you dress, it is important to look *soignée*, or cared for. In other words, you have given thought and attention to your skin, your hair, your clothes, and your accessories. French men and women are far less likely to "slop around" in public, and that includes vacations and making a quick trip out to the store for bread.

On the whole, you cannot overdress for a French social occasion. Dark suits and good shoes for men, and simple but elegant dresses and shoes for women are acceptable for cocktails and dinner parties. If a French host or hostess says, "don't dress up," it doesn't mean you can wear jeans and a T-shirt, unless the jeans are freshly pressed

Armani and the shirt or blouse is Yves St. Laurent or Christian Lacroix.

One notable thing about French people, male and female, is their preparedness to appreciate elegance and style in others. So complimenting women by saying "*Vous êtes très élégante*" ("You look wonderful") is considered polite rather than a come-on. One Frenchwoman confided that the best love affair she ever had lasted thirty seconds. It was the look a man gave her as she walked into Galeries Lafayette in Paris!

La Politesse

French men will stand if a lady enters the room for the first time, and will always open the door to let her through first. French women get up to greet another woman. During a meal, keep your hands on the table, not in your lap. Children are taught not to put their elbows on the table. A French friend was living in England. Her mother came over from Paris to visit her and noticed her daughter was sitting with her hands in her lap. She immediately said, "*Chérie*, you have lost your manners!"

Of course, you may find some of these protocols restrictive, and may not follow them at all. However, it is important to remember that the French abide by a kind of relaxed formality while entertaining, both at home and out, and that the higher up the social scale you go, the more pronounced it is.

LANGUAGE

Your passport into French society is your ability to speak good French. Your absolute priority for living in France, or visiting the country on a regular basis, should be to improve your knowledge of the language. The French language is the pride of France, and the French like you to speak it well and correctly. They will feel much easier with you, and you with them.

The biggest language schools in France are those of the Alliance Française (founded in 1883), which is devoted to the propagation of the French language and culture, and the Berlitz organization, which has over sixteen schools in France. Many universities run courses in French and French culture, and there are a number of conversation classes organized by groups such as *Parler Parlor* (held at the Berlitz schools but not run by them). One of the advantages of French and French culture courses is that they give you the basic historical and social knowledge that French children learn at school, and that is the background to much conversation.

There are things you can do to practice your French even outside the classroom. A key issue is getting accustomed to the rhythms of French speech, and that can be done only by listening—TV, radio, videocassettes, and audios are all good for listening practice. The important thing is to let the words wash over you to see if you can understand the general topic, rather than trying to understand every word. Later, try to pick out figures, dates, and names of places and people. French people often speak very fast, but don't get discouraged. You will gradually notice improvement in your ability to understand conversation.

Reading is another important skill. Don't try *Le Monde* or Victor Hugo to start with. Pick up flyers in the supermarket, or look at the headlines in *Paris Match*, *Voiçi*, *Elle*, or *VSD* magazines. Once again, don't expect to understand every word. Try to get the gist of it, and only look up key words.

For speaking skills, try talking to yourself. Describe everything you can in French, and go through your daily routines or shopping lists, speaking it all aloud. This will help to improve your confidence.

A dictionary is a vital addition to your household, kept where you can quickly refer to it. Use it every day to check new words. For many years *Harraps Shorter English-French Dictionary* has been the mainstay of many families. The French equivalent is the *Dictionnaire Robert*.

Asking about words and phrases is a great conversation starter. Use your learning as a conversational gambit. If your efforts produce laughter, laugh along—and learn. Those around you will get used to asking you how your studies are progressing, and to helping you with new words and phrases. Your efforts will be appreciated.

Shyness

The French value eloquence and flair in conversation, and pride themselves on being good conversationalists. But many French people are shy too, and, like you, have to make an effort to speak. It's important to try to make a contribution, and one way to practice conversation may be to repeat to yourself what you hear people say when you are out and about, such as in shops.

Make Friends with Your Local Shopkeepers

France is a relationship-based culture. In other words, people will take the trouble to serve you better if they know you, even just a little. Visit your local shops regularly, and get to know the butcher, baker, hardware merchant, and so on. The extra custom and attention will please them, and they will therefore want to please you, and to make sure you have the purchases you want. This is as true in a *quartier* of Paris as it is in a village in Provence.

THE ART OF CONVERSATION

Although much of French life revolves around
food, conversation is almost as important. "*Le
grand repas*" (the all-important long family meal)
can last several hours, and is also the opportunity
for a long conversation. The French enjoy
discussing all subjects in depth, from sports to
philosophy, from politics to movies. Discussion
lengthens everything, from a trip to the
supermarket to a chance meeting in the street to,
above all, lunch.

Conversation can be lively. People speak
volubly, and gesticulate. They interrupt each other
frequently, and quick exchanges are the rule.
Sometimes the conversation seems aggressive to
outsiders, but not to the French, who are brought
up to be competitive. They have a satirical sense
of humor, and witty remarks are common, but
turnabout may not be fair play. People can be
quite touchy, and pride may be easily hurt.

Foreigners may appear dull to the French, not because they have nothing interesting to say, but because they take too long in saying it. Brevity is the soul of wit and for the French,  wit itself is the art of conversation. So it is important not to go on talking for too long. The French are always checking to see if they might be boring you, and you should do the same for them!

Be careful if you're using French, or even English, about the use of slang. It may come across as being vulgar. Also, it is rude to speak with your mouth full!

Although no subject is really taboo, talking about money is not welcomed, and to ask a person how much he or she earns, or how much has been paid for a certain item, would be extremely impolite.

As in many countries, mention of certain historical periods may cause distress, particularly wartime experience. Discussion of the Second World War and the shifting allegiances of that time may be painful or embarrassing for older members of a group, and broaching the subject of the more recent Algerian war may raise unpleasant issues of colonial racism and the trauma of decolonization. Be sensitive to the vibrations around you.

Hal Wilson, a sculptor, ran into local sensibilities when, after six years in France, he was commissioned to submit designs for a monument to the local heroes of the French Resistance against the Germans in the Second World War. He created a "winged victory" statue, which was admired by the council but rejected by the mayor, who called it Communist-inspired and made of rubbish. Eventually the statue was erected in a nearby village controlled by a left-wing mayor. Apparently the mayor at the original proposed site believed that the pro-German government of Marshal Pétain at nearby Vichy was Catholic, unlike the Godless fighters of the Resistance. All this took place sixty years after the end of the Second World War! "Fais-gaffe!" ("Watch out"), as the French say.

chapter five

THE FRENCH AT HOME

THE HOME

The French home in a town or city is usually an apartment, and is usually rented. Walk along a French street, and you will see a continuous row of buildings of four or five stories with a large wooden or metal door at intervals along the street. Ring the bell outside that door, and it will open to allow you into a courtyard. Around this courtyard will be elevators or staircases up to the apartments.

Most such apartment blocks were traditionally presided over by a *concierge* (caretaker), usually a woman, who occupied a ground-floor flat and was responsible for distributing mail and cleaning the stairs and hallways. The *concierge* was a figure of myth and legend in French life and literature. In reality she was the guardian of the block, and kept an eye on all comings and goings.

Nowadays you press the intercommunication button of the apartment you want, and state your name; an internal button will open the *porte cochère* (literally, carriage entrance) to let you in. Sometimes the *porte cochère* is operated by a code.

If you don't know it, use your cell phone to contact the person you are visiting to find it out. Otherwise you could be waiting for a long time.

The public interior of the building may bear no relation to the opulence of the apartments inside. Electricity is expensive in France, and most corridors are lit by timed lights that tend to go out at the most inconvenient moment. As you go upstairs or along corridors, look ahead for the light switches or buttons so that you can find them easily if the lights go out.

French apartments vary from huge suites of rooms to the little top-floor or attic studios (one-room apartments) often called *chambres de bonne* (maids' rooms). For a nation obsessed by food, kitchens are often surprisingly small, and they are private. Wandering into the kitchen to continue the chat with your host is not done in France.

Second Homes

Many town-dwellers have second homes in the countryside, or maternal or paternal houses in the provinces. Because so many country-dwellers are moving into the towns, cottages in small villages are available quite reasonably, and are being snapped up by French people and foreigners alike as *résidences sécondaires.*

The dream of every Frenchman and woman is to have a house and garden built to their own specifications. Not everyone can do this, of course, and even if you do find your dream home in Brittany you are restricted to local building materials and styles.

Houses

Outside the cities, people live in houses and villas of great variety. There is a strong tradition of regionalism in France, and people on the whole like to live near their relatives and to keep in touch with their roots.

Furniture and Furnishings

French houses are leased or sold without fixtures and fittings, so it is possible to find yourself in a house or apartment with no light fittings, cupboards, shelves, or toilet paper holders. If moving into a new house or apartment, check first with the real estate agent, because finding appliances that exactly fit the holes in the walls can be hard.

Le Bidet et la Salle de Bain

In France the bathroom (*salle de bain*) and the toilet are usually the same room. You will also find, next to the toilet, a low basin with taps and an inverted shower arrangement, called a *bidet*. This is used by women for more intimate cleansing. In the movie *Crocodile Dundee*, Paul Hogan finds a *bidet* in his suite in the UN Plaza Hotel in New York. His costar, Linda Koslowski, soon set him right as to its correct use.

You should also be aware of *le lavabo turque*, which is a hole in the floor, with small platforms for your feet, over which you stand or squat. Foreigners are often repelled by these, which have largely been replaced by flush toilets, but be prepared for them in some of the older and more basic rest stops, such as on expressways.

Privacy

In her book *Cultural Misunderstandings*, the French author Raymonde Carroll described her shock at finding Americans, "living in the street." By this she was referring to American houses being exposed to the street, with small front gardens and no hedges, and curtains kept open at all hours. French houses, by contrast, are much more enclosed, separated from the street by walls and hedges, and with curtains always closed in the early evening to protect the privacy of the family. Again, this reflects the great wish of the French to keep their home and family life private.

THE FAMILY

French and Anglo-Saxon attitudes toward bringing up children are somewhat different. The Anglo-Saxon family is devoted to individualism, bringing out the talents and individual personalities of its children. The French family is devoted to bringing up children to be model family members and citizens who will conform to French society. Family relationships are tight, and adult sons and daughters will often stay close to their parents, dining with them every week and calling them every day. Building a social identity is more important than encouraging self-expression. French parents are no less loving and doting, but they do it in a different way. They believe that, for a child to be well brought up, certain basic attitudes and values need to be instilled, and like everyone else they worry about a potential breakdown in society that might threaten those standards.

Being *Bien Élevé*

Middle-class families bring up children strictly and without a lot of the freedom that American children enjoy. French parents don't necessarily feel that they have to stop what they're doing to listen to their children or indulge them. This is not psychological cruelty, but social induction. French children learn to choose the right time to speak, to be witty, to get attention. And they learn what it is to be *bien élevé* (well brought up) and *mal élevé* (badly brought up). Polly Platt, in *French or Foe?*, sums it up well when she says that French mothers don't hesitate to call attention to stupidity, bad taste, bad manners, boring comments, inappropriate reactions, and any lapse in appearance.

What is interesting is that, despite the pressures on the social system, the rise in one-parent families, the children born out of wedlock to couples living together, the competing needs of working women, and a more fragmented lifestyle, the system still continues.

Hierarchy in the Family

In the French family the husband is king and is the authority figure. As many foreign wives of French husbands testify, next in line to the throne is the mother-in-law, jealously overseeing her daughter-in-law's behavior and keeping a wary eye on how her grandchildren are being brought up. This can be particularly hard on American and British wives of French husbands.

French children do not on the whole raid the fridge at will, forget to tidy up, borrow the car without permission, talk back to their parents, or indeed treat the house as theirs and encourage their friends to do so. French parents can therefore be shocked at the freedom that some American and British parents give their offspring.

Key to the French family is a network of siblings and generations all living in the same area and in close touch, unlike the more fragmented and smaller American and British families. This creates a strong network of contacts and, of course, Frenchness that is much more cohesive than the looser systems of values and alliances of the Americans and British.

Of course there are "black sheep," and people living away from home, but the point is that in France this is seen to be a deviation rather than the norm, whereas in modern America and Britain a close family network bound by common behavior and values may be upheld by individual families, but is not a general social ideal.

Sexual Mores

France is reputedly a country of sexual libertarianism, and we have the cancan, the Folies Bergère, and the Pigalle to prove it. In fact, the average French family is much more conservative than the average American or British family. It is not uncommon for French girls to refrain from intimate sexual relations until well into their twenties, which may be one reason why French boys lay siege to American and British teenagers and those of other nationalities.

EDUCATION

For a French parent, education is everything.
The child must have as many and as important
certificates of academic attainment as possible. In
American and British business life, experience
counts. In French life the right education and the
right certificates count. This is why some
experienced American and
British teachers wishing to
work in France are horrified to
find their experience
downgraded because they do
not have the equivalent degree
certificate to the French one.

Most children go to a
nursery school before they are
six years old. Education in France is compulsory
from the age of six to sixteen, but most French
children leave at eighteen. Most parents send their
children to a state school (*école publique*), which is
free and considered to provide the best education.
Wednesday is a free half-day for schoolchildren,
depending on the school, but many have lessons
on Saturday morning. The system is very
competitive, and repeating a class is necessary if a
certain level has not been achieved by the end of
the school year. All children in France learn from
the same national curriculum, which prescribes in
detail what is to be taught.

Some parents choose to send their children to a private school (*école privée*). These are often denominational, most frequently Catholic, but follow the same national curriculum as the state schools. Private schools are under contract to the state, which pays teachers' salaries and contributes to the upkeep of the buildings. Fees are therefore low, and parents tend to choose their children's schools according to local convenience, reputation, and facilities rather than for religious reasons. In both state and private schools, all books, pencils, exercise books, and text books have to be bought by the parents. In a state or private boarding school (*pensionnat*) parents of students from low-income families can apply for grants (*bourses scolaires*) to help with equipment. Grants are also available for academic achievers.

The French take great pride in their long and prestigious literary tradition. However, in schools literature is not as important as mathematics, which is the traditional gauge of intelligence, perhaps because it demands logical thinking. Philosophy is compulsory for students in the upper secondary schools.

The French at School
La rentrée ("Back to school") in September is a national event as children join their classes with their *ardoises* (writing slate), hardbound

textbooks, and writing implements, and, of course, perfectly and fashionably dressed. French schoolchildren don't wear uniforms.

Every year, from the first year in school, children enter a *concours*—a public competitive exam. Their grades at the end of each academic year have to reach a certain level to avoid repeating the year (and seeing their friends move up without them).

Foreign children who join schools in France are not prepared for how hard the French children work at their studies. The school year runs from September to June, with breaks at Christmas and Easter, but there is great emphasis on learning and on thinking logically. This also means there is great emphasis on mathematics. U.S. and, increasingly, British education cultivates the opening of the mind, expression, and creativity. French education at the secondary level stresses the transfer of knowledge to form the mind and prepare it for society.

The French secondary-school leaving examination is the *Baccalauréat*, known as the *Bac*. To have the *Bac* at the right level assures free entry to university. Then, three or four years' study and attainment of the *Bachelier* (Bachelor's) and the *Maîtrise* (Master's) degrees leave you on the lowest rung of yet another ladder. Anyone with the *Bac* has the right to go to university, but there is also a tier of highly selective *Grandes Écoles*, where future top executives, civil servants, and politicians are educated. The *Grandes Écoles* are the basis of a lifelong network of people who are equally at home in government and industry and move easily between the two.

The Grandes Écoles

The *Grandes Écoles* are the pinnacles of the French education system. A *Grande École* sets you up for life. The closest U.S. comparison would be the Ivy League or MIT, or, in Britain, the universities of Oxford or Cambridge. Entry is by competitive examination, and, after four years of grueling study, successful graduation allows you the coveted title of Graduate of the *Grandes Écoles*, or of the ultimately prestigious *École Nationale d'Administration*, or ENA, or the *École Polytechnique*. If you graduate from the *École Nationale d'Administration*, you are an "*Enarque*." If you graduate from the *École Polytechnique*, you are an "*X*." As an ENA graduate you are destined for high office in government, the civil service, or industry or perhaps all three at different times in your career. Your academic certificate is your passport to your future. As an *Enarque* you are entitled to address other *Enarques* as "*tu*," and as an *X* you are entitled to walk beneath former classmates' crossed swords at your wedding and to write on invitations, "*ancien élève de l'École Polytechnique*" (former student of the *École Polytechnique*). In recent years the *Grandes Écoles* have been opened to foreigners in order to recruit the best minds, and the examinations (*concours*) can be taken in English.

The difficulty of getting into these schools by competitive examination, and the prestige accorded to students on graduation, cannot be overestimated. On graduation at age twenty-four you are made for life. In this way France creates a tightly knit elite that moves easily between government, the civil service, and business.

MILITARY SERVICE

Military service still exists in France, although nobody is actually drafted any more. Traditionally every young man over the age of eighteen had to do ten months' military service, or community service as an alternative. Boys were called up in front of a commission called the *rendezvous du citoyen* (citizen's rendezvous) and given a choice.

In fact, these days, being registered is enough and nobody actually does *SMA*, or adapted military service, as it is known.

DAILY LIFE

French daily life is dominated by the working week. People will be up around 7 a.m. to get the children to school and to commute to work, which starts at 9 a.m. The French day begins with coffee (often with milk), served in a bowl, not a cup, with bread, butter, and jam, or a *biscotte* or toast. School starts at 8:30 a.m. and finishes around 4:30 p.m. Lunch may be eaten at school, in the school cafeteria.

Although the tradition is diminishing in the big cities, the two-hour lunch is still important and 12:30 to 2 or 2:30 p.m. is a dead period. The working day usually ends at 6 p.m., but may extend to 7 or even 8 p.m. to compensate—*métro, boulot, dodo* (subway, work, and sleep) is how they used to describe it.

Shopping is an important part of the French day. The French like to buy small quantities of fresh food often, as well as buying basics and food for the freezer at the supermarket.

Evenings are spent at home, eating, watching TV, or preparing homework for the following day. The evening meal is eaten around 7 or 8 p.m.

It is during the weekends that the routine changes. The French admire hard work but not workaholics. The weekends are for relaxing, seeing friends, playing sport, eating and drinking, or just hanging out. Whoever is up first in the morning goes out to buy freshly baked bread and croissants for breakfast. Lunch is a leisurely affair, often with extended family members, preceded by an *apéritif* and a long meal followed by *digestifs* (brandy and liqueurs) and coffee.

For people who are fashion-conscious, it is interesting that the French dress quite casually. The trick is quality and style. Correctness of dress for the occasion is less important than the style of your clothes and the quality of the material and accessories. Despite having some of the best-known fashion logos in the world, the French are not obsessed by labels, but appearance is important.

chapter six

TIME OUT

The French work hard during the week, but weekends are the time for family, culture, and relaxation, and an opportunity to see friends, just hang out, and talk. The art of conversation is important, and time out gives them the opportunity to indulge it, whether it be puttering in the garden, working on do-it-yourself projects, going out, or eating and drinking with friends.

SHOPPING

The French like to enjoy themselves, and shopping in France approaches an art form. There are increasing numbers of supermarkets and hypermarkets (look for the names Auchan and Mammouth), but even these sell fresh local produce, and there are many small specialty shops. Chief among these is the *boulangerie* (bakery), open from 7:30 a.m.

until 7:00 or 8:00 p.m., baking and selling fresh
bread. The standard word for the long French
loaf is *baguette*, but you will soon learn that this
is just one of a range of breads of different
thicknesses and lengths that go by different
names. The *boulangerie* may also have *patisserie*
(pastries), including delicious strawberry or
apple tarts, cakes, and other delicacies.

Markets

The markets are as important as the shops. They
rotate around towns and villages, and you can
find out the market days from the local town hall
(*Mairie*) or tourist office (*Syndicat d'Initiative*).
Fresh produce is important to the French, and the
opportunity to pick up fresh fruit, vegetables,
meat, and cheese direct from local farmers is
valued. In Paris there are regular Saturday markets
in the squares of each *arrondissement*. Take a bag
with you. Plastic bags may be provided, but you
shouldn't expect it.

Markets are not just for food. There are
secondhand, antique, and junk markets (*marchés
de brocante*) and in Paris at the Porte de
Clignancourt is the famous flea market (*marché
aux puces*).

Markets of all kinds are the equivalent of the
U.S. shopping mall or British shopping center,
and are major social centers.

Banking Hours

Banks in France are open between 9:00 a.m. and 12 noon and 2:00 and 4:00 p.m. on weekdays, and from 9:30 a.m. to 12 noon on Saturdays. In certain areas they may be closed on a Saturday or a Monday. Banks are always closed on Sundays and on public holidays, although in big cities near the main station there may be a foreign exchange (*Échange*) booth open.

Some banks have a security airlock system between two entrance doors. Press the red button, and when it shows green the door will be unlocked. Repeat the process for the second door. Only one person can enter at a time.

LES GRANDES SPECTACLE

Grandes spectacles (great events) are concerts, galas, and displays. Advertised in the papers and on posters all around town, the *grande spectacle* is a major social event that might comprise a French or American star's open-air concert or a display of sports or dance. Jazz is very popular in France, and a major jazz festival is held at Antibes in the south every year.

Spectacles théâtrales are also popular and, for fans of classical theater, the Comédie Française in Paris offers regular presentations of plays by the classical playwrights Corneille, Racine, and Molière.

LE CINÉMA

Most French people see a film on average once a week, and the art of filmmaking is taken very seriously. The French film industry releases some twenty-five films annually. Government subsidies provide up to a third of investment capital, and films are commissioned by the state-run TV networks. In the largest cities many films are shown in VO (*version originale*), so you can watch films in English. For the French, and for an appreciative foreign audience, the French film industry is important and French films are well attended.

Every May filmmakers from around the world gather for the prestigious Cannes Film Festival in the south, and there is also an animation festival in Annecy.

CAFÉ SOCIETY

An important part of French society is the local café. Cafés sell alcohol as well as coffee, tea, and soft drinks, and people come for breakfast (*café au lait* and *croissants* or *brioches*) or for a lunchtime snack (*un pichet de vin rouge* and a *croque monsieur* or *croque madame*—cheese on toast, or cheese on toast with a fried egg on top), or simply for a cup of coffee and to sit and read the paper or watch the world go by. The café is a place to meet friends or simply to watch the football on TV. Cafés also offer sandwiches of *jambon* (ham), *fromage* (cheese), and *rillettes* (pork spread). If the weather is hot, try a *citron pressé* (fresh lemon juice) brought with a jug of sugar syrup for sweetening.

Le Café-tabac

Many cafés have a kiosk that sells cigarettes, lottery tickets, and Métro tickets, and also telephone cards, postcards, and stamps. They are usually indicated by a cigar-shaped red neon sign.

You will note that when you pay in a café or store, money and change are placed not in the hand but in a tray on the counter. This ensures that there is no doubt about how much money has been offered and how much change has been given.

Crêperies

For snacks, French people often go to a snack bar, café, or *crêperie*. A *crêpe* is a pancake, usually savory, filled with meat or vegetables and served with a salad. *Crêperies* also serve afternoon tea and cakes.

Just Hanging Out

Hanging out in one of the many sidewalk cafés is a particularly French pastime. As long as you buy a drink—coffee, tea, *citron pressé*, or *jus de fruits* (fruit juice)—you can sit for as long as you like, reading or just watching the passersby. The waiter may give you a glass of water on the side. That's also a reminder for him that you have ordered. When you are ready to go, call the waiter, pay the bill, and you're off to another café. If you're out in the open, you might be asked to pay first, and the waiter will tear your bill to show you've paid.

In most town centers (even Paris) things are fairly close by, and the sixteenth and nineteenth centuries are crammed together, so walking is a fascinating activity. On warm evenings around seven o'clock, especially in the south, you can join the parade as people dress up to walk along the central boulevards in the evening sunshine and show themselves off.

FOOD

A prime French concern is appreciation for the preparation and enjoyment of food and wine. It will not have escaped your notice that France regards itself as the world's center of fine cuisine. The appreciation of fine wine and good food is something that French children are brought up with, and that occupies a lot of time.

Restaurants

The French eat out a lot *en famille*, sometimes with friends and often with their dogs snuffling around between the tables. Trying a new restaurant or a new dish is a social experience to be enjoyed and then discussed in detail.

Interestingly enough, restaurants were invented in Paris in 1765 by a M. Boulanger. He made restorative brews for Parisians that he called "*ristorants*," and thus the word *restaurant* came into being. These quickly became popular social meeting places.

It is difficult for foreigners to appreciate that a meeting of French executives will give as much importance to a discussion of where to pick a certain type of mushroom and how to prepare it as to the share price of their company. In a business lunch, business discussion will normally be delayed until coffee is served. An educated palate is enormously important in France, and

Napoleon, who was famous for finishing a state dinner in twenty minutes and then leaving the table, is a notable exception. "Ah, but then he was a Corsican!" some French people will tell you.

French cuisine began to become a world standard by the eighteenth century. Auguste Escoffier, who was awarded France's highest honor, the *Légion d'honneur*, said, "to know how to eat is to know how to live." In France eating and drinking is akin to a spiritual experience.

Showing appreciation of food is important. The expression, "*Mes félicitations, Madame; votre repas est merveilleux.*" ("Congratulations, Madame. The meal is terrific.") will endear you to your host or local restaurant. People enjoy discussing food and wine and comparing the merits of different ways of preparing, eating, and drinking.

Two slightly gruesome examples will prove this. We know, for example, that before his execution during the French Revolution in 1793, Louis XVI had three soups, four entrées, three roast dishes, four sweet courses, fancy cakes, three compotes, three fruit dishes, Champagne, Bordeaux, Malvoisie, and port wines, followed by coffee.

In January 1996, President Mitterand died of cancer. Biographies record that a few days before his death he celebrated *le réveillon de la Saint Sylvestre* with his family and close friends and ate three dozen oysters, two *ortolans* (small birds) as well as *foie gras* and capon. Then he went back to Paris alone with his doctor and refused all food before his death.

WINE

Wine is the natural companion to food, and choosing and enjoying wine is an art. Wine should have the right color, smell, and taste, and should match the food of the different courses. A top restaurant will offer different wines with starter, main course, and dessert. *Rosé* (rose) or *blanc* (white) wine is served with starters, *rouge* (red) wine with main meat courses, dry white wine with fish and a sweet dessert wine with dessert. Etiquette demands that you wipe your lips with your napkin between wines and hold the glass by the stem so as not to prevent your full appreciation of the color and quality of the wine.

There are a number of wine areas in France, but traditionally the main differences are those of Bordeaux wines and Burgundy wines (both red and white). Burgundy wines are made from the Pinot Noir grape and tend to be slightly drier, and Bordeaux wines are made from the Cabernet Sauvignon grape mixed with a little Merlot. These tend to be fruitier and higher in tannin. The lighter Beaujolais wines of southern Burgundy are made from the Beaujolais Gamay grape, and the heavier Côtes du Rhône from a blend of nine different grapes. Also well known are the Muscadet white wines of the Loire Valley and the Gewürztraminer Riesling white wines of Alsace. Most famous of all is the sparkling white wine from the Champagne region centered on Rheims.

Wines are also graded as to quality. The top wines carry an *appellation contrôlée* label, but you can get very good *vins de pays* (local wines); many

southern wines are *vins de pays*, and it is worth
trying the local *vins de paille* (wines where the
grapes have been left to dry on straw in the sun).

One of the joys of traveling in France is the
opportunity to enjoy local wines and delicacies,
and the *Syndicat d'Initiative* or local restaurants
will usually advertise these. Many French people
remain intensely loyal to their local wines. Wine
will be served to children over the official age of
fourteen, and even younger children will taste
wine, watered down.

WHICH RESTAURANT?

The key guide to French restaurants is the
Michelin *Red Guide*, which lists restaurants visited
by its inspectors and awards one, two, or three
stars according to excellence. Michelin stars are
still very highly prized, both in France and
internationally. Another guide that has a good
reputation in France is the Gault-Millaut
Restaurant and Hotel Guide.

To build rapport with French colleagues, it is a
good idea to invite them to lunch—but let them
choose the restaurant and the wine. They will do
so sensitively, and will appreciate your discretion,
as you will enjoy the experience.

For yourself, if you are in a town, choose a
restaurant that is obviously full. That's where the

locals eat. There is a difference between the various kinds of restaurant, which, if you are traveling in France, you should know about.

Restaurants

These are open for both lunch and dinner, and are often closed on Sundays and Mondays, so it is important to check their hours and to make reservations. You are expected to eat three courses, and to order wine.

Brasseries

Brasseries are restaurants that are open all day and serve a limited number of dishes that are always available. If you wish, you can just order a main dish. In addition to restaurants and *brasseries*, keep an eye open for *Relais Routiers*.

Relais Routiers

Relais Routiers were originally truck stops, but they guarantee a full, good meal at a fixed price. Now if you buy the *Guide des Relais Routiers* and go into a restaurant with the *Relais Routiers* plaque, you are entitled to a full meal at the standard price. This is a smart way to eat economically and well.

Bistrots

Bistrots are small local restaurants. The name is a
loan word from Russian. Apparently Russian
Cossacks on leave in Paris in the nineteenth century
would rap on the table, shouting "*bistro!*"—
meaning "quickly!" So *bistrots* became places that
served quick, home-cooked meals.

If you simply want a quick meal in any
restaurant, order a *steak frites* (steak and chips).
You will be asked if you want your steak cooked
saignant (rare), *à point* (pink), or *bien cuit* (well
done). Unless you like your steak almost raw, go
for *à point*.

LUNCH AND DINNER

The French embrace the two-hour lunch
between about 12:30 and 2:30 p.m. This may
include a siesta in the south. Lunch and dinner
will follow the same pattern of *apéritif*, followed
by *hors d'oeuvres*, main course, salad, cheese, and
dessert. After dessert you will have coffee and
maybe a *digestif* (Cognac, Armagnac, or the local
eau de vie.) The demands of business and fitness
awareness are changing this routine, but
remember that the French invented *nouvelle
cuisine*. Rather than change the tradition of the
long lunch, they changed the food to include
simpler, lighter ingredients.

L'Apéritif

Before a meal you will normally be offered an *apéritif*. This might be water or a soft drink, but is usually alcohol, such as gin and tonic, *pastis*, such as Pernod or Ricard (aniseed drinks served with water), or a Martini. French people often drink a Suze (a bitter drink, like Campari, made with herbs).

Meals Etiquette

Meals in France are always accompanied by bread, which is eaten throughout the meal, except with soup, and which is never dunked, at least not in public. The exception is breakfast, where you may see French people dunking their *croissants* or bread in their *café au lait*. Don't cut the bread with a knife; break it with your fingers. Bread plates are usually not provided. Etiquette requires that you refrain from nibbling the bread until the meal actually starts.

Etiquette also requires that your hands and wrists, but not your elbows, should always be on the table. However, a quick head count in any restaurant will show you that many French people put their elbows on the table when not eating. Nevertheless, these rules are worth remembering if you are in polite society. The trick is to watch the natives and do as they do. This is particularly important when pouring wine and water. Usually the largest glass is for water.

Hors d'Oeuvres

In a top restaurant you may be offered, free of charge, an *amuse-bouche* (mouthwaterer) of fish or *pâté*, and sometimes, between courses, a serving of sorbet to clean the palate. Starters in a restaurant will normally consist of *crudités* (raw vegetables), *charcuterie* (cold meats), or shellfish.

Main Course

Although the pattern of a French meal doesn't vary, the content does. Normandy is famous for specialties cooked with butter and cream in cider and Calvados (an apple brandy). Burgundy is famous for dishes cooked in wine, Périgord for poultry preserved in its own fat, and *foie gras*, and Alsace for *choucroute* (sauerkraut). Provence, in the south, will offer dishes with olive oil, garlic, tomatoes, and peppers.

Vegetables may be served separately from the main course. There will be salt and pepper on the table, but you are not encouraged to use them: this would suggest that the chef has failed to season the food properly.

Salad, Cheese, and Dessert

Salad may follow the main dish, and then cheese always precedes the dessert. Usually up to three different cheeses are taken, and it is customary to clean the palate with a mouthful of wine before changing cheese. The meal ends with dessert, ice cream, or fruit, and is followed by black coffee, or maybe a *tisane* (herbal tea). At the end of the meal, a *digestif* (brandy, or a liqueur) may be offered.

Drinks

Wine is the traditional table drink. Usually, a table wine is sipped right through the meal. It is considered very bad form to get tipsy. To avoid your glass being refilled, always leave some wine in it. Bottled water is also served, either still (*non-gazeuse*) or fizzy (*gazeuse*). The most common bottled waters are Badoît (fizzy) and Évian (still), although the still water may vary according to the local source. If you want tap water (fully drinkable) ask for *une carafe d'eau.*

Wine is served by the bottle or half bottle (*une bouteille,* or *un demi bouteille*) or by the *carafe. Carafes* are available in 1 liter (1.1 quarts), 75 centiliters, 50 centiliters, and 25 centiliters. If you are on your own, ask for un *pichet de vin* (a small pitcher) or *un quart* (a quarter). This gives you a glass and a half. If you are with someone, *un demi* is probably enough, but in a group of three or more *une carafe de maison* (carafe of house wine) is appropriate. In France, *vin maison* (house wine) is always acceptable.

Prices

French restaurants generally display their prices outside. If prices are not shown, you can safely assume that the restaurant is very expensive. Most restaurants will offer a fixed price *ménu touristique*, or *ménu gourmand*—which is not for greedy people, but for people who like good food!

Tipping

In most French restaurants and cafés the bill will be marked "*service compris*." This means that service is included in the price. If it is marked "*Service non compris*," then you are expected to add 10 to 12.5 percent of the total to the bill. Even if service is "*compris*," it is common to round up to the nearest Euro, and leave the change on the plate.

LA VIE CULTURELLE: MUSEUMS AND ENTERTAINMENTS

If you are in Paris, buy *Pariscope* every week and turn to the back, where a section called "Time Out," published by the British *Time Out* publishers, will tell you in English what's playing. You can also access *Pariscope* on the Web at www.pariscope.fr and plan your visit. Opera lovers can book tickets in advance through the Web. Posters on walls and telephone kiosks advertise local events and films.

Museum opening times are listed in the main guides and also in the papers. It is worth checking there, as local museums are frequently closed on  Mondays, and national museums are often closed on Tuesdays, or sometimes on Wednesdays, or they may list their last admission time as earlier in the day than you might expect.

Almost all French museums and sights charge an admission fee. It is generally possible to buy a ticket that allows you admission to a number of additional local museums and sights. The value of this ticket is that it gives you immediate access, avoiding lines.

Visiting Churches

Apart from the major tourist attractions of the great cathedrals such as Notre Dame in Paris, Chartres, and Rheims, churches throughout France can be a mine of cultural experience, with historical frescoes, paintings, and architecture, and, since they are open for prayer, are absolutely free. Churches often offer organ recitals and free concerts, especially in summer.

THE ART SCENE

Art and culture are very accessible. Local artists hold *vernissages* (openings of exhibitions) with a group of friends where, with a glass of wine in your hand, you can meet and talk to other guests. One weekend a year, usually the third weekend in September, is designated *Les journées du Patrimoine* (Heritage days). On these days many of France's treasures are open to the public free, or at a reduced rate. Museums or stately homes often offer a *visite insolite*, an opportunity to go behind the scenes and see treasures not normally shown to the public. Once again, the *Syndicat d'Initiative* will have the details.

LA VIE SPORTIVE:
LEISURE AND SPORT

The French are very enthusiastic about sports, and in addition to international sports such as football and rugby, they are fond of cycling and skiing. The famous cycle race, the Tour de France, takes place in July. The winner of each stage wears the coveted yellow jersey. Many French take a week off in winter to go skiing in the Alps or the Pyrenees. Water sports such as windsurfing and jet skiing are popular along

France's varied coastline in summer. Even village squares are used for sports. Go out in the early evening and you will see a group of people (usually men) playing *boules*, throwing iron bowls either to get as close as possible to the *cochonnet* (piggy), a wooden target ball, or to dislodge their opponents' bowls.

The French Ministry of Tourism invests heavily in providing information and facilities. The *Syndicat d'Initiative* in each town will advise you of things to do and see locally, and you will also find signboards advertising such attractions. A recent initiative is to explore the inland waterways in a hired boat.

For walkers and cyclists there are ample opportunities and facilities to enjoy the countryside. There are *Auberges de la jeunesse* (youth hostels) and *Campings* (camp sites) at many tourist spots. Hire a bicycle: northwestern France is quite flat, and it's interesting to explore outlying villages and Celtic remains.

LE PIQUENIQUE AND *LE CAMPING*

The French are great outdoor enthusiasts, and picnicking and camping—both done in great style!—are very popular. Expressway "*aires*" provide excellent facilities for picnicking. Campsites with impeccable facilities are often to be found in the most beautiful places in France.

TRAVELING

DRIVING

Because of its size compared to its population,
France is one of the pleasantest countries in
Europe to drive around. It has a well-maintained
network of toll expressways (*péages*), highways
(*routes nationales*), and minor roads. It feels,
outside the main cities, fairly traffic-free, but
French drivers can drive very fast. In France you
drive on the right, and speeds and distances are
measured and given in kilometers.

The speed limit is 80 mph (130 kmph) on
expressways, 56 mph (90 kmph) on the roads, and
31 mph (50 kmph) in built-up areas. French drivers
don't always observe these limits, and will often flash
their headlights at cars coming fast in the opposite
direction to warn them of police speed traps.

Expressways in France are mainly toll roads.
As you enter, either you pay a few coins or you
collect a ticket and pay at the other end. The
routes nationales (N roads) run parallel to the
toll roads and are free, as are the narrower D
roads, or *routes départementales*.

On the *routes nationales* and the *routes départementales* there are circular intersections, or roundabouts. Traditionally in France priority is given to traffic entering these from the right, but increasingly traffic on the roundabout takes priority. Many now have signs warning you that *Vous n'avez pas la priorité* (you don't have priority), and to *Cédez le passage* (yield).

As for pedestrians, French drivers are not very considerate. Even where there are pedestrian crossings it is unwise to march out, confident of your right of way. Consequently, to calm the traffic, increasing numbers of speed bumps are being introduced into built-up areas, and these are hard enough and high enough to damage a car's suspension if driven over at speed too often.

Those driving in France are compelled by law to carry certain things. One is a red warning triangle that must be erected behind the car if you have to stop because of an accident or a breakdown. Another is a Red Cross first-aid pack, so that minimal first aid can be administered after an accident. Finally, in the case of drivers of cars imported from Britain, dimmers must be placed over the headlights so as not to dazzle oncoming drivers at night, and each car must carry a spare set of headlamps in case of failure. If the police stop you for any reason, you may be fined if you do not have these items.

Getting gasoline (*essence*) is not difficult. France has a mixture of self-service (credit card) and garage-hand assisted stations. Elf Acquitaine, the state-owned gas-company, has its own service stations. There are three types of gasoline, *supercarburant* (high octane, lead replacement), *sans plomb* or *superplomb* (both unleaded), and *gasoil* (diesel). *Supercarburant* is indicated by a blue pipe (in the United Kingdom it is red).

As it is by far the largest city in France, Paris is the greatest driving challenge. The one-way system can be irritating, and the shortage of parking is frustrating. French drivers park in the smallest spaces and make use of their bumpers to enlarge the space between parked cars. In the center, parking spaces are metered, with high prices to discourage commuters from using their cars rather than public transport. August is the only time when driving is easy in Paris, as that is when most people have gone away on holiday.

Paris has a ring road surrounding it, called the *Boulevard Périphérique.* It is the best way of avoiding the center of Paris, but it also gets crowded in the rush hours between 7:00 and

9:00 a.m. and 4:00 and 8:00 p.m. If you are driving on the *Périphérique* and are unsure of your exit, be sure to stay in the right-hand, or exit lane. Normally, you will be given a 3-mile (5000-meter) and a 0.6-mile (1000-meter) warning that you are approaching your exit.

There are two periods when main roads should be avoided. These are the weekends either side of July 31/August 1 and August 31/September 1. The French holiday month is August, and whole factories and firms close down for the month. At the beginning and end of it the main roads are clogged. The expressway south to the sun from Lyon is crowded with cars piled high with camping gear and bicycles or encumbered with trailers and caravans, and everyone is jockeying for position, stressed and hot tempered, with the inevitable breakdowns further holding up the already crowded traffic. It is not a good time to be a foreigner on French roads, and to the French themselves the RN 1 (*Route Nationale 1*, running north-south) is considered a death trap. Other dangerous times on the roads are the national holidays of July 14 and August 15.

The wearing of seatbelts is compulsory, and it is illegal to have a child in the front seat even if strapped in or on a passenger's lap. The French police apply the law rigorously, especially in the case of drinking and driving, and can withdraw a driving license on the spot in the case of drivers found over the limit. On the other hand, they can be especially tolerant toward foreigners driving foreign cars. If you stop at a snack bar on the expressway you will be served only nonalcoholic drinks, including nonalcoholic beer, unless you are also buying food.

To avoid traffic congestion, the French police try to offer alternative itineraries. In operation "*bison futé*" they invite French holidaymakers to try different routes advertised by "*bison futé*" signs. These are also explained on French TV and radio.

Car rental
Car rental in France is the same as anywhere in the world, and you need to show your international driving license and your international insurance certificate (green card).

Fines
In France you can be fined on the spot for speeding, and you also lose points off your license. Fines are usually paid in cash, but you have twenty-four hours to report to the local *gendarmerie* if you only have your credit card.

AAA equivalent
The equivalent of the AAA in the United States and the AA in Britain is *l'Association Automobile*, which

has reciprocal arrangements with its U.S. and U.K. equivalents. Check this out before you leave.

Insurance
Check that you have medical insurance valid for France; in the case of accidents, hospital treatment can be very expensive.

SNCF

Many travelers in France will use the train system—SNCF, *Société Nationale des Chemins de Fer* (the National Railway Company). The SNCF is a very efficient system, with clean trains and comfortable seats. The express train (*train corail*) even has a special carriage where children can play and, in summer, live entertainment may be provided at no extra charge. A carriage can become a cinema, an exhibition hall, or a showcase of regional specialities.

You can book tickets in advance through the Internet at www.SNCF.fr through the French Minitel system (see Chapter 9: Communications) and at the stations. Before boarding a train you must validate your ticket by pushing it into a

small machine that punches a hole and stamps the
date. There are frequently ticket inspectors on
trains, so get it right to avoid an instant fine.

One of the great advantages of traveling in
France is the TGV (*train à grande vitesse*) system,
which offers high-speed links from Paris to the
regional capitals. Tickets for these must be booked
in advance and all seats are pre-allocated.

GETTING AROUND IN PARIS

The Métro
The easiest way of getting around
Paris is on the Métro (subway
system). Métro stations are
identified in the street by a large
"M." On the Métro you need
only one ticket, whatever the
length of your journey. To
avoid lines at ticket
offices (*guichets*), you
can buy your Métro
tickets in a *carnet* of ten tickets. Newsagents and
cafés-tabacs also stock them. You can use your
Métro ticket on the Métro, on buses, and on the
RER (see below) within the city limits. If you are
traveling to Paris from the United Kingdom by
Eurostar, you can also buy Métro tickets at the

exchange bureau in the departure lounge. This is a good way to avoid long lines for tickets at the Gare du Nord.

Each line takes its name from the last stop, so on your return journey the line will have a different name (the name of the last stop in your new direction). If you have to change, follow the sign saying *correspondance* (change) and head in your new direction.

If you are staying for a while in Paris it is a good idea to apply for a monthly *carte orange* (orange card), which gives you the right of travel on bus, Métro, and RER within the city. You'll need to apply for a form at the ticket office of your local station and to supply two passport photographs signed on the back.

Buses

Some visitors refuse to go by Métro, preferring to see the sights as they travel. You can buy a bus route guide that shows clearly which bus goes where, and where to change. To validate your ticket, board the bus and have your ticket punched by a machine in the front or the middle of the coach. Be aware that polite standing in line for buses is not a French virtue. Once again you can use Métro tickets on the buses. Line 72, which goes from the Hôtel de Ville (Town Hall) and takes in the Eiffel Tower, is a particularly good sightseeing route.

RER *(Réseau Express Regional)*

This is the Paris suburban train system.
Partly underground and partly above ground,
it is the best way of getting to Disneyland
or Charles de Gaulle Airport from the center
of Paris; it has limited stops at key central
points and intersects with main line
stations and with the Métro. Once again,
you can use your Métro tickets within the
city limits as RER is managed by RATP (the
Métro line).

Once on the platform you will see a timetable
on the wall. Trains are identified on the front by
strange names such as NEMO or TALE. There
is also a signboard on the platform showing
which stations are served by the train
(*stations desservies*).

Tickets

Hold on to your ticket. You will need it to
enter and sometimes to leave the RER and the
Métro, and also for occasional ticket inspections
on the train.

Rush Hour

Métro and RER rush hours in Paris are 7:00 to
9:00 a.m. and 6:00 to 7:30 p.m. These are times
to avoid taking large backpacks, heavy luggage,
and baby strollers, if you have a choice.

WHERE TO STAY

The French hotel industry is clearly rated according to the facilities offered, from one to five stars. Two-star hotels can be very basic, but acceptable, and reasonably cheap. Guidebooks will advise on the best hotels in each area. Usually you pay a set price for the room rather than per person, and breakfast is usually not included. Some hotels have a restaurant attached.

Chambres d'hôtes are bed and breakfast establishments, and may also offer *table d'hôte*, which is an evening meal.

If you are staying longer, think about renting a *gîte*, or self-catering holiday cottage. These are often old cottages that have been renovated and are interesting and comfortable places to stay for a week or more. *Gîtes de France*, the organizing body, also runs the *chambres d'hôte* system.

Caught Short

If you are traveling, you will occasionally need a toilet. These usually carry the sign "WC" or "*toilettes.*" Men's and women's toilets are usually indicated by a picture or occasionally by H (*Hommes*) and F (*Femmes*), or, more traditionally M (*Messieurs*) and D (*Dames*). Public toilets may be available, but you are best served by going into a café to use its facilities, and you should then order a drink or at least leave a small tip. Some toilets have an attendant by the entrance who expects a tip in return for keeping the booths clean and equipped.

Remember that in rural France the *toilette Turque*, where you squat with your feet on porcelain platforms either side of a hole, still exists.

Finally, for admirers of old France, the free-standing public urinals, known as *pissoirs*, have been removed from the streets and replaced by unisex *cabines*, which are cleaned automatically. Green and red lights have replaced the *libre* (free) and *occupé* (occupied) signs, and you need a 1-Euro coin to enter.

TRAVEL ABROAD

Some 80 percent of French people take their annual holidays in France. Others take their holidays abroad, where they will meet mainly French people. These are the famous Club Mediterranée holidays, founded in the 1950s by Gérard Blitz and aimed at providing exotic vacations for French people. Today the clientèle of Club Med is very international, and there are Club Med holiday resorts in the south of France itself. For a good travel experience and great holiday facilities, you could do worse than join them.

chapter eight

BUSINESS BRIEFING

BUSINESS AND GOVERNMENT

The link between French business and government is very close. It is so close, in fact, that government ministers may be parachuted into industry, and businessmen into government. The French have a word for it: "*pantoufler.*" *Pantoufles* means a pair of slippers. Both Socialist and Conservative ministers may shuffle between the two. Part of the reason for this is that leading French government and industry figures will have had the same education, graduating from the prestigious *Grandes Écoles*.

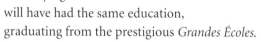

Traditionally, a key role of central government was to protect French industry. This has been modified by EU rules, by decentralization, and by privatization. One effect of decentralization has been that decisions on local production plants are made by the local *département*, city or commune. The local chamber of commerce now often acts as an intermediary between foreign and local businesses, instead of a *notaire* (lawyer/public notary), whose rates are fixed by the government and whose services are more expensive.

As the state becomes more aware of the pressures on the public purse caused by its huge stake in national and infrastructure enterprises, there have been increasing moves to privatize parts of state industry and to set up joint ventures with foreign companies.

Finally, EU rules have discouraged protectionism and encouraged, to some degree, a greater openness to foreign investment.

As France privatizes, modernizes, and deregulates, what has been the effect on the French style of management?

FRENCH BOSSES

French managers are, above all, technocrats. They are the charismatic leaders of their companies, highly educated, and masters of the technical and organizational detail required to run their companies. A French manager will expect to have at his or her fingertips operational information that American or British managers would expect to look up when needed or only know at a "ballpark" level. French managers are very concerned with the details of the process, whereas American and British managers may be more concerned with the results.

The head of a French company is the PDG, or *Président Directeur Général*, and he or she exercises absolute control over the company. The French PDG is expected to be authoritarian in style and to run the company with flair and accuracy. PDGs may be quite aloof from management colleagues. Their authority is based on education and competence, and all the important decisions will be taken by them.

A key factor in French business is a commonality of background. As pointed out, many PDGs will have been in government at some point, and will have attended a prestigious *lycée* and graduated from one of the *Grandes Écoles*.

This leads to a very strong sense of hierarchy and formality in French companies. In teams, differences in hierarchy are respected and upheld, and informal socializing between the boss and junior colleagues is uncommon. This can surprise more democratically minded American and British colleagues.

The hierarchical style has repercussions on efficiency. Managers may not delegate, and staff may feel demotivated. One disgruntled English manager in a French firm said he was called to meetings only to receive instructions. There was no discussion of ends, ways, and means.

Yet, one of the values of charismatic management is the ability of the manager to motivate staff by getting them to "buy into" his or her own personal vision. When staff recognize that the rationale for a project is sound and that their input is valuable, then they will work very hard.

Decisions made at the top are not always made quickly. There may be time-consuming arguments about the relative rationales behind different systems, and the arguments may focus on intellectual consistency rather than on pragmatic or creative solutions. The French are suspicious of risks and of easy solutions, and again this may slow things down.

WOMEN IN MANAGEMENT

Although most women in France work, and professional equality between the sexes is required by laws passed in 1972, women still earn only 75 percent of their male counterparts' salaries; they also hold France's lowest-paid jobs, and two out of three earn the minimum wage.

Women are moving into middle management, but the pressures of career (long lunches and late-night meetings) militate against balancing family and job. On the other hand, France is very women-friendly in terms of providing generous maternity benefits and leave. Women are tending to marry later, around twenty-five years old, and also to stay in the work force, often with part-time jobs. Women with three or more children receive a state-funded pension.

Sexual harassment at work is a crime, and, according to a law passed in 1992, men accused of it can be fined and sentenced to up to a year in prison, but the law applies only to hierarchical superiors. On the other hand, the traditional *galanterie* toward women in the workplace still exists, and women exploit it. Elegant dress and style are part of a woman's armory in business.

MAKING CONTACT

Initial contacts in France are quite formal, and will be done by letter, but don't expect a secretary to make an appointment on behalf of her boss, as she may not have the authority to do so.

Appointments are rarely made outside office hours. These are usually from 9:00 or 9:30 a.m. to 6:00 p.m. Sometimes the boss may stay late and make an appointment for after 6:00 p.m. You may find that an appointment, once made, is later changed or cancelled when another matter is seen as more important, and takes priority.

It is important to remember that the month of August is sacrosanct as a holiday for French businesspeople. Don't expect to sign contracts or schedule business meetings during August.

An American publishing firm was in negotiations for a major publishing deal with a French firm. The contract was ready for signing at the end of July, and the U.S. executive prepared to fly over for signature, only to be informed that his French counterpart was departing south for his annual family holiday. Eager to make the deal, the U.S. publisher insisted his French colleague delay his holiday by a week or fly back to Paris for the day to sign the contract. He flew to Paris and cooled his heels in an empty city for a week. The French publisher never turned up. The contract wasn't signed, and the deal was never resuscitated.

On the whole, French people still prefer to do business with other French people. It is not enough, however, just to do the business: it is very important to create a good long-term relationship, and this is the main focus—becoming part of the network. Therefore, as a foreigner, you need to create trust, if possible through a common interest or passion. This may mean that discussing business takes second place to building the relationship.

FORMALITY

The protocol of French business is firm. You are expected to dress smartly, shake hands with everybody, and use formal titles correctly.

You will also find the French style of business writing to be extremely formal. Letters may take a long time to arrive. For quick responses it is best to use e-mail or telephone.

It is interesting that, in recruitment, French managers set great store on good handwriting: rounded, elegant, and even. A handwritten CV is an important means of gauging a candidate's overall suitability for a job.

Getting Around The Rules

As a country with a civil code dating from the nineteenth century and a penchant for elegant, logical, and rational administrative regulations, how do the French get around these to solve insoluble problems? They use what is known as *Système D*. *D* stands for *débrouillard* (being able to get around problems). *Système D* covers the system of finding the bureaucrat who is prepared to bend the rules, or to find a precedent or special case (*cas particulier*) that can be applied to your own case and allow you exemption. It is never illegal, but is always intensely practical, and is the equivalent of similar ways of getting around bureaucracy in many Latin countries. Recognize it, but don't refer to it.

RULES FOR BUILDING SUCCESSFUL CONTACTS

Do Your Homework
French managers expect to have operational details, theirs and yours, at their fingertips, and so should you. Familiarize yourself with organigrams—facts and figures of your organization and their organization—and any historical information that is relevant to your discussions. They will expect to do the same.

Don't Expect Business First
The French are very business-minded, but the relationship is important. They may feel it would be valuable to engage with you on intellectual subjects, ranging from history to theology. It is a way of gauging the kind of person you are and the extent of your education and intellectual

ability. Remember your discussion skills and discussion topics from university. In extreme cases this could go on for several meetings. Be patient, and keep the door open.

Go To The Top

French business is hierarchical. Aim for the decision-maker. Make sure the person you deal with is your direct counterpart in the French organization. By the same token, don't expect to discuss technical details with lower-ranking managers. Get someone else in your own organization to do that.

Take Your Time

The French do not like to feel rushed. Make sure you take the time to build the relationship with your French counterpart.

> A French HR manager asked thirteen companies to bid for a large training project. All thirteen companies responded, and she rejected ten of them. "Only three followed up by asking to come and see me," she explained. "One of those lectured me on how I had got the tender proposal wrong, so I didn't want to work with them. So I have two companies to work with." It was by initiating a personal relationship that these two training companies got the business.

Boredom Is The Killer

The French are noted for having the shortest attention span of any people in Europe. If you find you have lost their attention, find a quirky or controversial issue to spice things up. On the other hand, lively and intense discussion means they are deeply engaged and involved. Contrary to what you might think, the more they interrupt, the more involved they are likely to be.

Don't Go Informal

If a business card is offered, demonstrate interest and respect. Take a brief look at it, making sure the relevant contact numbers are on it, and put it in your wallet.

Elevators and doorways can cause socially awkward moments. Women enter first, obviously, but afterward seniority takes over. If you are the senior person present, expect to go through the door first.

American and British people, generally impatient with formality, sometimes make the mistake of starting to be informal with French colleagues with whom they have formed a superficially good working relationship. This can meet with a chilly reception. If you are speaking French, always use the "*vous*" form, and retain *Monsieur* and *Madame* until it is appropiate to do otherwise.

Don't Blame People

Always objectify problems. "Houston, we have a problem," is always better than "You made an error." Failure and blame are taboo in French management. Identify a problem and indicate that it can be sorted out. On the other hand, bringing a problem to their attention and excusing yourself for doing so is guaranteed to ensure a sympathetic and positive response. Remember, even if it's their fault in your eyes, the French will normally seek a way of casting blame somewhere else.

Diplomacy First

The links between government and business are not there for nothing. The French are masters at diplomatic negotiation, and have been for hundreds of years. Allow them the time to display their diplomatic skills, and use yours as well. One key to diplomacy is that price comes last, not first. It is considered vulgar to mention money too early in the proceedings. Establishing the relationship is always the first aim.

TIME, AGENDAS, AND DEADLINES

These are three things that the Americans, and increasingly the British, consider sacrosanct that are not regarded in the same way by the French. Timing is flexible, within limits. For the French it

It's Not My Fault

A French visitor knocked over and broke a Japanese Imari plate in a colleague's office. His response was not, "Sorry, let me pay for replacing that," but "What a place to put a valuable plate! It could so easily be knocked over!"

It's Not My Problem

In another case, a French colleague forgot to pick up a visitor arriving on Eurostar from London at Paris Gare du Nord to take him beyond the Périphérique to a meeting near Versailles. When the visitor called him on his cellphone his first response was, "But I'm not meeting you till the fifteenth." "But it is the fifteenth," the visitor replied. "*Mon Dieu!*" said the Frenchman, "I haven't got my car." Rather than immediately arranging for a cab, he said, "Get a train, and I'll see you at the meeting." To his credit, when they eventually met, after the visitor had endured an hour's tedious and confusing journey, the Frenchman did say, "Sorry."

is more important to discuss an issue thoroughly than to keep to schedule. Things move at a slower pace to allow for relationship building. If a meeting runs long and someone else is kept waiting, he or she will understand.

The same attitude extends to keeping to the agenda. The French regard all the items on an agenda as linked, and treat agendas simply as guidelines, not to be followed rigidly, and above all not to be timed.

In the same way, deadlines are not sacrosanct for the French. If a deadline is important, then it must be clearly stated and checked. The rule is, don't expect; inspect—but gently. The French make a distinction between a general target (*date cible*) and a final deadline (*dernière limite*). Taking your time is equivalent to prudence. The French won't insist on deadlines if there are good reasons for delay, and they expect you to be equally understanding.

During takeover negotiations of a French company, the British C.E.O. was impressed by the tight agenda drawn up by his French colleagues. On learning about the French attitude to agenda keeping, he asked, "So was that just for my benefit?" His sales manager wryly nodded.

FRENCH NEGOTIATING STYLE

The French are brought up to believe in logic. For them it is important to construct a logical argument with total clarity, consistency, and precision. They appreciate abstract argument and well-thought-out projects, and rely on consistency rather than on pragmatism, which is often at odds with the American and British style.

At a meeting it is important for everybody to contribute to the discussion. This is considered thorough and thoughtful. The final decision may be made outside the meeting, but once made is firm. In contrast, American and British negotiators like to agree in principle at a meeting, but to review and adjust the details subsequently. The French do not understand why the British, in particular, seem to agree to something at the end of the day, and then appear to want to renegotiate it at the following meeting.

The First Contact

We've already seen that making contact with French companies can take time. Even if you get a quick phone response, it does not imply commitment, and getting personal commitment is everything. A letter or fax does mean something. Your French counterpart is assessing your business validity, your educational background, your philosophy of life, and your general style. Your experience and background are as important as, and may be more important than, your commercial proposal. To this end, if at all possible, you should be introduced by a colleague known to the company you are contacting or, failing that, by your embassy or chamber of commerce.

If you do send a letter of introduction, don't expect an immediate reply, and don't ask for one. A correspondence is like a relationship. It flows and has pauses. You may have to send a number of letters before you get a positive reply.

Cold calls may get a frosty reception from firms unused to dealing with American and British companies. People often use the phone to complain, or to divert complaints. French people much prefer making to receiving business calls.

A telemarketing executive cold-called the head office of a major international company in Paris, having been given a contact name there by the manager of one of the company's subsidiaries in London. At first, the French respondent claimed not to know the British contact. Then, after listening briefly, he said, "No, no, Madame, we do not do things like that here," and put the phone down.

When the contact is made, do not assume that the first meeting will be cordial. It will probably be polite but noncommittal. Your French counterpart will be concerned to establish his or her own status and control over the meeting. The atmosphere may seem cooler than you expect, having made the effort to make contact.

It will pay dividends if you can express yourself in French. If you use an interpreter, try at least to introduce yourself in French. Don't discuss family and friends, but discreetly let your French counterpart know your academic status and contacts. Don't expect agreement, action points, and time frames at a first meeting. But do write a follow-up letter, thanking your counterpart for meeting you, and also suggesting the next meeting. If a meeting is prolonged, or if you are invited to lunch, then you are in. But don't expect it. Continuity of contact is the key to building a successful relationship. Getting the next meeting is the name of the game.

Negotiating

Most people find negotiating with the French quite difficult. One cause is the French approach to negotiation. Whereas most parties come to a negotiation with a degree of common ground, and the negotiation is about what can be achieved at what price, the French tend to approach matters from logical first principles and take a "Why should we be doing this?" approach. This means that exchanges of position papers prior to a meeting may not be taken into account during the meeting. Proposals are built up slowly, logically, block by logical block, with each stage analyzed and discussed. This means long debates, and that nothing can be taken for granted. As a result, foreign negotiators often find their schedules disrupted and their emotions ruffled by having to go back to basics. Hard-sell techniques won't succeed here. The important thing is to remain calm and to enter into the spirit of the discussion.

It is vital to present your own argument logically, carefully evaluating the positive and negative points. Negative points should be admitted, but balanced and outweighed by the benefits. Your flair in presentation will be appreciated. The logic of your argument is important. French negotiators will point up an error in logic in the afternoon where there is a difference from what you said in the morning.

POINTS TO REMEMBER ABOUT MEETINGS

Preparation

A man should wear a traditional, dark blue suit. For a woman, elegance and flair are important. Your presentation needs to be very well prepared, and you should be able to argue every point. Take nothing for granted. Have the details of your company and their company at hand. Make sure you are able to analyze the benefits, rather than simply sell them. Keep your presentation clear and concise.

Maintain Status

Aim to establish rapport, and to agree to broad lines of cooperation. As the discussion leader, don't take notes. Your assistant does that. Lawyers and other staff will iron out the details. However, be prepared for further meetings to deal with issues arising.

Appreciation

As a senior French executive once said, "a company is not a democracy." It is, however, quite paternalistic. A French manager will value your appreciation of the modernization he or she has achieved in the company's operations, or the facilities provided for the staff. A humane working environment is important to the French, and that involves creating a space where people want to stay working for a long time.

Subtlety

The French appreciate a subtle approach. They respond to analysis, not to hard sell. A suggestion that there may be an alternative supplier rather than a statement that "We are looking elsewhere," may get a better result. The French prefer debate rather than aggressive questioning. They react adversely to direct criticism, and it is important to focus on the problem, not on the person who may be responsible for it.

Consistency Is All

In a business meeting the French listened politely to the American presentation in the morning. In the afternoon discussion, the American said something that made the French start. "But Monsieur, in your presentation this morning you appeared to say something different." Half an hour was spent on clarifying the link between the apparent contradiction between the morning's and the afternoon's comments. The lesson is, intellectual consistency is everything.

CONTRACTS

When drawing up contracts, the French side will insist on precision. A verbal agreement is only a preliminary to a written agreement, which alone is legally binding. As long as the written documents have not been signed, nothing can be considered final.

The French may wish subsequently to adjust the terms of a contract according to circumstances, but will normally not expect to extend the same courtesy to others.

MEALS

The French are Latins, and believe that food and drink are important in creating and cementing relationships. The person who is trying to secure the contract pays for the meal. And reciprocating hospitality is important. "Going Dutch" is not a French concept.

chapter nine

COMMUNICATING

FACE TO FACE

Greeting People

You're in France, at a party or at a business meeting. First impressions count for the French, so handshaking and visual contact are important. Smiles are not necessary, and don't be surprised if you don't receive one.

We have seen that one should not just say, "*Bonjour.*" "*Bonjour, Madame*" or "*Bonjour, Monsieur*" is the correct greeting. And, of course, never use "*tu,*" except to children. Always use "*vous.*" The French stand on ceremony, and even if you are speaking English, it pays to remember that and to cultivate, at least at first, a certain reserve.

Many French people have double first names, such as Jean-Claude or Jean-Paul or Marie-Louise, so be prepared for that. If you hear this, the name is "Jean-Claude" not "Jean."

What Shall We Talk About?

It is important to speak well. The French like stimulating conversation, and they like to feel you are *au fait* with what's going on in the world. Use the Internet to be aware of news, current events, and gossip, and look at the headlines of newspapers to see what people are talking about. As the French say, "It's not enough to be witty. It's important to use it wittily." So how you say things can be as important as what you say. A startling insight or opinion will make people sit up and want to talk. If you're not feeling witty today, don't worry. Interest in intellectual matters and a willingness to discuss them, or to take an interest in your host's views, is all that matters. A very successful British fund-raiser swore that all he needed in France to promote a conversation was two words, "Oh really?" which encouraged his host to carry on talking about his favorite topic for hours while appreciating the fund-raiser's informed knowledge of the subject!

The French will talk happily about their wine collections, restaurants, or sports, and will be interested in your impressions of France. However, there are a number of topics, acceptable in American or British conversation, that the French on the whole prefer to keep to themselves.

Families

For the French, the family is private. Don't talk about your family, and don't ask about theirs, unless your host brings it up. Family pets, especially dogs, may be a different matter.

Age and Salary

It is considered bad manners to talk about your age and salary, and even about your company's turnover.

Politics, Religion, and Health

General discussion is fine, but how you vote and when and where you go to church, as well as discussion of your illnesses and your analyst, are considered too personal.

Humor

The French sense of humor depends on wit and word play. The British sense of irony largely escapes them. Charm is infinitely better than humor. It travels better. Above all, avoid telling sexist, racist, or dirty jokes.

Don't Mention the War

There are two of them. The Second World War, and the Algerian War of Independence; and one could add a third—the French war in Indochina. Unpleasant things happened to families in all of these, and old wounds can unwittingly be stirred in the most innocuous conversation. That being said, the French love talking about politics. Any negative comments, however, will be reserved for your political system rather than theirs! Globalization, particularly, can be an emotive subject.

Once again, these are general guidelines. Be ruled by the person you are talking to, but if you are pitching first, avoid these areas of discussion. As in all French conversations, keep it short and light. French people constantly comment on the American and British habit of going on too long and monopolizing discussions. Chatting, interrupting, being interrupted, and moving along, are the hallmarks of a successful conversation.

BODY LANGUAGE

Everybody knows that the French talk with their hands. Gesticulation is the norm, and it gets more noticeable the farther south you go. The French tend to stand closer to each other than American or British people. Where the Anglo-Saxons prefer a distance of two feet, the French are comfortable with one. Smiling is not something the French do readily, unless there is genuinely something to smile about. They tend to find the general bonhomie of Americans, and some British, phony and therefore to be distrusted. A dignified reticence is your best bet. Similarly, an over-relaxed posture is a sign of bad upbringing. Sitting up straight, not slouching, and keeping your feet and elbows off the table are all considered important, although many French people will now happily put their elbows on the table during breaks in a meal. The trick is always to appear perfectly in control of your body and your emotions.

As a certain control over the body is appreciated, so with the voice. French children are taught not to raise their voices, and to speak loudly in public is to show bad upbringing. Speaking clearly is appreciated; raised voices and shouting are not. So if you are accustomed to expressing yourself forcibly and at high volume, tone it down.

LA LANGUE FRANGLAISE

As we have seen, the French language is one of the glories of French civilization, and the Académie Française goes to great lengths to preserve it from outside attack—particularly from Americanisms, advertising jargon, and computer software terminology. It is important to remember that French was once the world diplomatic language, and the French do not want it forgotten in the *hégémonie Anglo-Saxon.*

From time to time a war of words erupts in the French press about how the use of English is destroying the French language. This can have

SOME FRENCH GESTURES

Counting
Starts with the thumb, not the index finger.

Pointing
Not done. Indicating is done with the open hand. Asking for a lift is also done with the open hand, never the thumb.

Yawning
Cover your mouth with your hand. Also do so when using a toothpick, and turn your head away. Use a handkerchief if you are sneezing, and if you have to blow your nose in public you should also turn your head away.

Beckoning
Done with the palm of the hand down, all fingers toward you. Don't use palm up and one finger. To call a waiter, do it by eye contact and a little wave.

Thumbs up
Shows approval. The American "Okay"—rounded forefinger meeting the thumb—means "worthless" in French.

Shrugging the Shoulders
This is a typical Gallic gesture that conveys a negative reaction, meaning "So what?" "Whatever," "I don't care," "Nothing to do with me," or "This is ridiculous." It signifies that no useful communication can be achieved on this topic.

I'm Fed Up
As the most easily bored people in Europe, the French have various ways of indicating that they have had enough. A hand wiped across the forehead, the fingers flicked across the cheek, staring straight ahead, or even playing an imaginary flute, can all indicate that it is time to change the subject.

Other Signs
To show that food is delicious, the French may kiss their fingertips. To tell you someone is crazy, they may put their index finger to the side of their head, as the British do. To show they don't believe you, they may pull one cheek down with the finger below the eye, to mean, literally, "My eye!" or "I don't believe you."

practical implications in the prosecution of
companies using English words in their
advertising. All contracts by law have to be written
in French and, since 1994, advertisements,
product labels, instructions, and public signs
must be in French (or be translated into French if
a foreign language is displayed).

Commercial Consequences
The English natural cosmetics firm The Body
Shop was fined in 1996 for marketing products
using the terms "no frizz" on a hair treatment
cream, and "pineapple" on a facial cleanser. Be
aware, therefore, that not "doing your homework"
could cost you money.

Standard French is not the only language
spoken in France. Twenty-one percent of French
people claim to understand or speak a regional
language. Alsace has a German dialect, and the
south of France has the Provençal dialect, as well
as Catalan, Spanish, and Basque. Corsica speaks
an Italian dialect and, in the west, Brittany has
Breton, and many more local dialects.

In addition you will hear Arabic spoken by
North African immigrants as well as the languages
of other countries.

POSTAL AND ELECTRONIC COMMUNICATION

Post Offices

Post offices in France are called *bureaux de poste* and are open between 8:00 a.m. and 7:00 p.m. on weekdays, and until 12 noon on Saturdays. In villages and towns they may be closed between 12 noon and 2:00 p.m. for lunch. The postal system is reasonably efficient. You can also buy stamps from *Cafés-tabacs*, marked with a red cigar sign. French post boxes are painted yellow.

Addresses

Each of the areas of France is denoted by a code that is used on letters and in car registration numbers. Paris, for example, is 75. Towns are divided into districts or *arrondissements*, also numbered. So, in Paris, 75008 denotes the eighth *arrondissement* Incidentally, this is a very good address, being just down the road on the Champs Elysées from the Arc de Triomphe.

Usually the addressee's name is written with the title in full, not abbreviated, and sometimes with the surname preceding the first name. Be prepared for both.

In a town or city an apartment might be shown on a letter as *Apartement no. 3 au troisième étage à gauche*, which means apartment no. 3 on the third floor on the left. *Gauche* is left and *droite* is right. The street name follows, preceded by the number, for example, *8 Rue de Berri*, and the number of the city and its name last. So a letter addressed to someone in Paris might look like this:

Madame Francine Dufour
Apt 14 à gauche
8 Rue de Berri
75008 Paris Cedex
France

Cedex, or CEDEX, stands for *courrier d'entreprise à distribution exceptionelle*, a special delivery service for business mail.

Telephoning

In 1997 the French telephone system was upgraded. Telephone numbers now have ten digits, including the area code of the region you are in. So the code for France is 33 followed by 1 for Paris, 2 for the west, 3 for the east, 4 for the southeast and Corsica and 5 for the southwest. If you have a ten-digit number you need add nothing. If you have an eight-digit number you need to add the area code (*indicatif*) of the region. Within France, add 0 (for example, 01 for Paris). To dial from outside France, dial 33 (country code) and then the area code without 0, followed by the number.

To dial out of France, dial 00, followed by the country code of the country you are dialing.

If you are calling a Freefone number (*numéro vert*), the number will begin with 008, and if you are calling a cell phone number it will normally begin with 06.

Public Telephones

If you are using the public telephone system in France you will find telephone boxes in even the smallest villages. However, all the coin-operated telephone booths have been withdrawn and you will need a telephone card or *télécarte*. *Télécartes* are available from post offices and *café-tabacs*, and you should buy either a 50- or a 100-unit card.

To find a telephone number, use the telephone directory (*Bottin*) or the Yellow Pages (*Pages Jaunes*) for businesses. In post offices the *Bottin* has been replaced by the *Minitel* system, which you can consult free of charge.

Minitel and *Le Web*

The French are good at gizmos, and the comparatively slow takeup of the Internet in France was a surprise to many. Part of the reason was the Minitel, a minicomputer installed in French post offices and offices, which provided instant electronic access to a range of services such as train and airline bookings, directory enquiries, and theater, cinema, and restaurant bookings.

Now the French are fully on the *courrier électronique* system with e-mail, called "*le mel*" and the Web, known as "*la toile*" or "*le Web*." Web surfers are known as "*internetantes*."

CONCLUSION

To foreigners France has always seemed contradictory. Visitors over several centuries have expressed the same ambivalent love and admiration, combined with annoyance and frustration. Mark Twain quipped that "France has neither winter, summer, nor morals. Apart from that it is a fine country." The American traveler John W. Forney wrote in *Letters from Europe*, published in 1867, that "to change from England to France is almost the transition from one planet to another." But France is also a contradiction to the French. The late President de Gaulle is reputed to have said, "France has no friends, only interests." The philosopher Voltaire wrote in a letter in 1777 that, "The French will always be partly tigers and partly monkeys." The great Napoleon himself observed, "The French complain of everything and always," but that

"It is easy to govern the French through vanity." Comments such as these reflect both the French sense of style and show, and the careful and calculating self-interest of the people.

Wise travelers in France have learned to love this contradiction, and to enjoy the beauty and sheer intellectual and sensual excitement of the country and its main cities. That sense of rules being made to be broken, of barriers being set up to be knocked down, gives an irresistible sense of liberation to all but the most hidebound visitor. In France, that most formal of European nations, you feel that anything is possible. And sometimes it is. In the emerging international community of nations, France, as a pillar of the growing European Union, will continue to make a major and distinctive contribution.

Resources

Alliance Française
101 Boulevard Raspail, 75006 Paris.
Tel. 01 42 84 90 00
*The leading French state-funded organization for studying
French language and culture.*

American Club of Paris
34 Avenue de New York, 75116 Paris.
Tel. 01 47 23 64 36
Cultural and contact center for U.S. citizens resident overseas.

Association of American Residents Overseas (AARO)
BP 127 92154 Suesnes CEDEX
Tel. 01 42 04 09 38
Aid and contacts for U.S. residents in France.

Lions Club International
295 Rue St Jacques, 75005 Paris.
Tel. 01 46 34 14 10
*Charity and cultural organization running events for
members in France.*

Rotary Club, Paris
40 Bd Emile Augier, 75116 Paris.
Tel. 01 45 04 14 44
*International charity organization running events and
contacts for overseas residents.*

WICE (Women's Institute for Continuing Education)
20 Bd de Montparnasse, 75015 Paris.
Tel. 01 45 66 75 50
*A nonprofit cultural and educational association providing
courses, services, and resources for members. Serves the
English-speaking community in and around Paris.*

YMCA/YWCA
33 Rue du Naples, 75008 Paris.
Tel. 01 47 20 44 02
*Sports and accommodation facilities for overseas residents
and visitors. Centers throughout France.*

Further Reading

Ardagh, John. *France in the New Century*. London: Penguin Books, 2000.

Asselin, Gilles and Mastron, Ruth. *Au Contraire*. Maine: US Intercultural Press, 2002.

Baillie, Kate and Tim Salmon. *The Rough Guide to France*. London: Rough Guides, 2001.

Carroll, Raymonde. *Cultural Misunderstandings*. Chicago, Illinois: University of Chicago Press, 1990.

Cole, Robert. *France: A Traveller's History*. Moreton-in-Marsh, Gloucestershire: Windrush Press, 2000.

Gendlin, Frances. *Living and Working in Paris*. London: Kuperard Publishing, 1998.

Gray, Jeremy, et al. *Lonely Planet: France*. Melbourne/Oakland/London/Paris: Lonely Planet Publications, 2001.

Hampshire, David. *Living and Working in France*. Fleet: Survival Books, 1996.

Jack, Andrew. *The French Exception*. London: Profile Books, 2001.

Johnson, Diane. *Le Divorce*. London: Vintage Books, 1997.

Joseph, Nadine. *Passport France*. St. Rafael, California: World Trade Press, 1997.

Knorr, Rosanne. *The Grownup's Guide to Living in France*. Berkeley, California: Ten Speed Press, 2000.

Lewis, Richard D. *When Cultures Collide*. London: Nicholas Brealey Publications, 2000.

Mole, John. *Mind Your Manners*. London: Nicholas Brealey Publications, 1993.

Platt, Polly. *French or Foe?* London: Culture Crossings, 2002.

Stern, A. Z. and Joseph A. (eds.). Reif. *Everyday French*. London: Kuperard, 1999.

Taylor, Sally Adamson. *Culture Shock! France: A Guide to Customs and Etiquette*. Portland, Oregon: Graphic Arts Center Publishing, 2000/London: Kuperard, 2000.

Zeldin, Theodore. *The French*. London: Harvill Press, 1983.

French. A Complete Course. New York: Living Language, 2002.

French Without the Fuss. New York: Living Language, 2002.

culture smart! france

Index

culture smart! france